W9-CNA-710

A Portrait of

LUXEMBOURG
THE GRAND DUCHY

LUXEMBOURG,
le grand-duché

LUXEMBURG,
das Großherzogtum

LUXEMBURG,
het groothertogdom

PHOTOS AUFNAHMEN PHOTOGRAPHS FOTO'S
VINCENT MERCKX

TEXTES TEXTE TEXTS TEKSTEN
GEORGES-HENRI DUMONT

A Portrait of

LUXEMBOURG
THE GRAND DUCHY

LUXEMBOURG,
le grand-duché

LUXEMBURG,
das Großherzogtum

LUXEMBURG,
het groothertogdom

VINCENT MERCKX
EDITIONS

Couverture : le lac de la Haute Sûre
Pages 2-3 : les collines de la vallée de l'Our
Pages 4-5 : Esch-sur-Sûre
Pages 6-7 : les rochers du *Binzeltschlëff* dans le Müllerthal
Pages 8-9 : la vallée de la Moselle du haut du Scheuerberg

Umschlag : der Obersauersee
Seiten 2-3 : die Hügel des Our-Tals
Seiten 4-5 : Esch-an-der-Sauer
Seiten 6-7 : die Felsen des *Binzeltschlëff* im Müllerthal
Seiten 8-9 : das Mosel-Tal vom Scheuerberg aus gesehen

Cover : The Haute Sûre lake
Pages 2-3 : Hills of the Our valley
Pages 4-5 : Esch-sur-Sûre
Pages 6-7 : The *Binzeltschlëff* in the Müllerthal
Pages 8-9 : The Moselle valley from the heights of the Scheuerberg

Kaft : het meer van de Boven-Sûre
Pagina's 2-3 : de heuvels van de Ourvallei
Pagina's 4-5 : Esch-sur-Sûre
Pagina's 6-7 : de rotsen van het *Binzeltschlëff* in het Müllerthal
Pagina's 8-9 : de Moezelvallei van op de Scheuerberg gezien

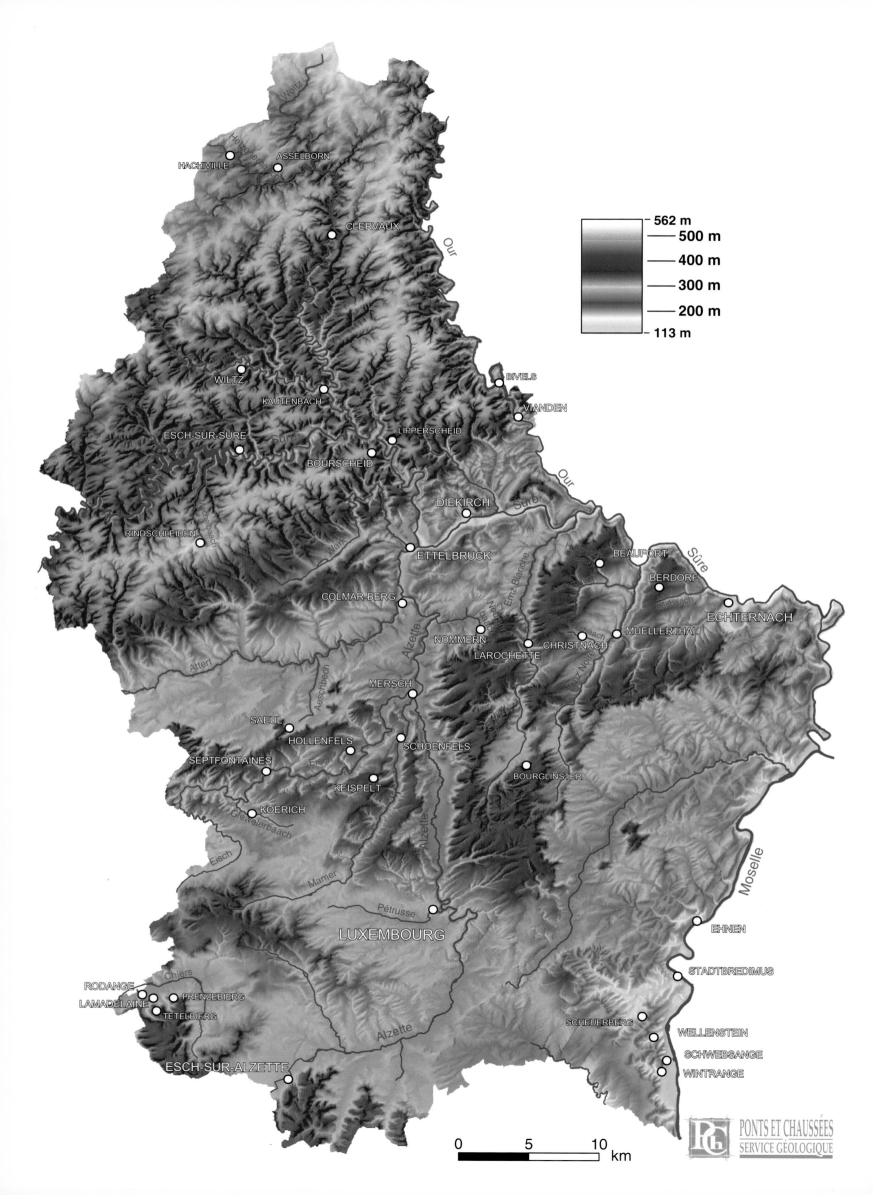

HACHIVILLE
ASSELBORN

CLERVAUX

Wiltz

Our

WILTZ
KAUTENBACH

BIVELS
VIANDEN

ESCH-SUR-SURE
Sûre
LIPPERSCHEID

BOURSCHEID
Our

Sûre

DIEKIRCH

RINDSCHLEIDEN
Wark
ETTELBRUCK
BEAUFORT

BERDORF

COLMAR-BERG
Enz Blanche
MUELLERTHAL
ECHTERNACH

Attert
NOMMERN
LAROCHETTE
CHRISTNACH

Alzette
MERSCH

Aeschbech

SAEUL
HOLLENFELS
SCHOENFELS

SEPTFONTAINES
Eisch
BOURGLINSTER

KEISPELT

KOERICH
Gleiweierbaach

Alzette
Eisch

Mamer

Pétrusse
Moselle

LUXEMBOURG

EHNEN

RODANGE
Chiers
STADTBREDIMUS

LAMADELAINE
PRENZEBIERG

TETELBIERG
SCHEUERBERG
WELLENSTEIN

Alzette
SCHWEBSANGE

ESCH-SUR-ALZETTE
WINTRANGE

562 m
500 m
400 m
300 m
200 m
113 m

0   5   10
km

PONTS ET CHAUSSÉES
SERVICE GÉOLOGIQUE

Table des matières · Inhaltsverzeichnis · Table of contents · Inhoudstafel

Voyage dans les temps géologiques
Eine Reise durch die Erdzeitalter
A Journey Through Geological Time
Reis door de geologische tijden

Souvent, dès la fin de l'été, les crêtes de l'Oesling retiennent les nuages bas prisonniers des vallées humides aux versants abrupts et boisés. C'est le cas près de la Sûre en aval de Bourscheid.

Ab Ende des Sommers halten die Kämme des Öslings die niedrigen Wolken in den feuchten Tälern mit ihren bewaldeten Steilhängen gefangen. Dies ist in der Nähe der Sauer fluss-aufwärts von Bourscheid zu beobachten.

Towards the end of summer the crests of the Oesling, rising above the steeply sloping, wooded and humid valleys, often hold fast the low clouds as can be seen here near the Sûre, downstream from Bourscheid.

Op het einde van de zomer houden de bergkammen van de Oesling de laag hangende wolken vaak gevangen in de vochtige valleien met hun steile en beboste hellingen. Dit is het geval bij de Sûre, stroomafwaarts van Bourscheid.

LE grand-duché de Luxembourg partage non seulement son histoire mais aussi ses paysages avec ses voisins. Le Gutland, ou *Guttland* en langue luxembourgeoise, est bel et bien le prolongement oriental de la Gaume et septentrional de la Lorraine. De même, l'Oesling ou *Éislek* appartient au massif que l'on nomme Ardenne à l'est et Eifel à l'ouest. La démarcation entre ces deux régions naturelles – Gutland au sud et Oesling au nord – est nette à plusieurs égards : les roches qui constituent le sous-sol, la forme des vallées creusées par les rivières, la faune et la flore qui s'y sont développées, le mode de vie de leurs habitants…

Une ligne joignant Roodt à Fouhren délimite ces régions aux substrats rocheux fort différents. Dans la partie septentrionale, un socle datant de l'ère paléozoïque (c'est-à-dire de -540 à -250 millions d'années) et, dans la partie méridionale, des couches de couverture datant de l'ère mésozoïque (de -250 à -65 millions d'années). L'Oesling, comme le Massif schisteux rhénan, fait partie de la chaîne de montagnes dont les restes s'étirent des Ardennes françaises au Rhin ; le Gutland quant à lui forme le Golfe de Luxembourg, à l'extrémité nord-est du Bassin parisien.

Les roches de l'Oesling se formèrent il y a quelque 390 à 380 millions d'années à partir du dépôt de couches de boues et de sable au fond d'une mer. Les géologues appellent cette époque le Dévonien inférieur. Ces strates de roches sédimentaires furent ensuite plissées au cours de *l'orogenèse hercynienne* il y a environ 350 millions d'années, lors de laquelle les sédiments se transformèrent en ardoises, schistes, grès quartzeux, quartzophyllades et quartzites tandis que s'élevèrent de hauts sommets. Puis la jeune chaîne de montagne, démantelée par l'érosion, disparut peu à peu, ne laissant qu'une vaste pénéplaine aux faibles élévations située presque au niveau de la mer.

Il y a 225 millions d'années, cette surface d'érosion du massif dévonien fut à nouveau submergée par la mer. Celle-ci progressait d'est en ouest, pour s'ouvrir plus tard vers le sud et le sud-ouest et former une vaste étendue marine dont le centre fut le Bassin parisien. Le socle paléozoïque fut alors en grande partie recouvert par les dépôts du début du Mésozoïque. Dès la fin du Mésozoïque, la mer se retira définitivement de nos régions. Le paysage sera ensuite remodelé par l'érosion et par le soulèvement à la fois plus rapide et plus important de l'Oesling par rapport au Gutland.

De la Haute Sûre à l'Our

Le paysage actuel de l'Oesling est marqué par un plateau qui s'élève en général à cinq cents mètres d'altitude. Ce haut-plateau, très vaste au nord-ouest et généralement couvert de pâturages et de champs, perd de son étendue vers le sud et le sud-est où il est fortement déchiqueté par les vallées encaissées de la Sûre, de l'Our inférieure et leurs affluents. Les dénivellations entre les fonds de vallée étroits et les replats y dépassent souvent la centaine de mètres : à Vianden, le château perché sur un éperon rocheux à trois cents mètres d'altitude domine l'Our d'une centaine de mètres (voyez la photo aux pages 136-137 ci-après) tandis que, tout proche, le bassin de la centrale électrique est creusé à cinq cents mètres d'altitude au sommet du Mont Saint-Nicolas. Les versants abrupts sont couverts de forêts ; exploités pour leur bois, les résineux y remplacent souvent les taillis de chênes dont l'écorce fournissait le tannin à l'industrie du cuir.

Le réseau hydrographique de l'Oesling est principalement formé par la Sûre et ses affluents septentrionaux. La Clerve, notamment, recoupe sur son cours du nord vers le sud les trois grands plis qui traversent la région du sud-ouest au nord-est : l'anticlinal de Bastogne, le synclinal de Wiltz et l'anticlinal de Givonne.

En aval de Clervaux, la Clerve traverse des grès et des quartzophyllades, roches plus dures et plus anciennes qui affleurent sur le flanc méridional d'un grand pli en forme de selle : l'anticlinal de Bastogne. Plus au sud lui succède un pli en forme de gouttière, le synclinal de Wiltz constitué de schistes plus tendres, formant une légère dépression au relief moins accidenté ; de Drauffelt à Lellingen, la vallée de la Clerve est alors moins étroite, ses versants moins abrupts. Enfin, la rivière rencontre les formations plus dures du flanc nord de l'anticlinal de Givonne et, jusqu'à Goebelsmühle, les vallées sont à nouveau particulièrement encaissées.

L'orientation des méandres des rivières de l'Oesling suit souvent la direction des couches géologiques et des nombreuses failles et fissures. Les éperons rocheux bien dégagés y constituent des emplacements privilégiés pour les châteaux : citons Clervaux, Esch-sur-Sûre, Bourscheid, Vianden.

Le paysage de cuesta

Une coupe dans le sous-sol nous montre que le socle dévonien, affleurant dans l'Oesling, se prolonge vers le sud où il est cependant recouvert par les formations plus jeunes du Gutland. Cette couverture mésozoïque du nord du Gutland débute au Trias inférieur, il y a environ 225 millions d'années, avec les couches gréseuses voire conglomératiques. Plus au sud-ouest, des couches de plus en plus jeunes se superposent, la dernière étant les calcaires du Dogger déposés il y a 175 millions d'années, que l'on trouve près de la frontière française.

Dans ce paquet de couches presque horizontales, qui plongent de quelques degrés vers le centre du Bassin parisien, alternent roches résistantes – grès, calcaires, dolomies… – et roches tendres, surtout les marnes. Cette alternance est à l'origine du paysage de *cuestas*. Celles-ci se sont formées par l'érosion plus ou moins rapide des différentes couches au cours des derniers millions d'années : la roche dure constitue le front de la cuesta, à forte pente, la formation tendre recouvrant le revers à faible pente. Les deux cuestas les plus marquées sont celles du Grès de Luxembourg, datant du Lias inférieur, et du Dogger.

Au nord du front de cuesta du Grès de Luxembourg, qui s'étire entre Beckerich, Mersch et Nommern, l'avant-pays marneux est exploité par l'agriculture tandis que le front gréseux est couvert de forêts de feuillus. À Nommern, le village se trouve dans l'avant pays marneux alors que les Nommerlayen (page 92) constituent le front gréseux, le plateau légèrement incliné vers le sud formant le revers de cuesta recouvert de marnes plus jeunes.

La cuesta du Dogger prolongée par la Côte de la Moselle en Lorraine, a un front double formé de deux couches résistantes, la Minette et les calcaires du Dogger, séparées par une formation plus tendre et de faible épaisseur. Le Prënzebierg avec son ancienne mine à ciel ouvert (pages 45 à 47) ainsi que le Tëtelbierg sommé de son oppidum trévire (page 24) font partie de la cuesta du Dogger. Ils s'avancent un peu plus loin dans l'avant-pays car l'érosion y a été un peu moins rapide.

Les trois collines qui précèdent le front de cuesta près de Differdange, le Zolverknapp qui culmine à 422 mètres, le Loetschet et le Packebierg, matérialisent la ligne de partage des eaux entre les bassins mosellan, c'est-à-dire l'Alzette, et mosan, la Chiers. Celle-ci coule au pied de la cuesta et quitte le Luxembourg vers l'ouest. Elle est l'unique cours d'eau luxembourgeois qui draine vers la Meuse. Tous les autres rejoignent tôt ou tard la Moselle.

L'Alzette, du sud au nord

En suivant le parcours de l'Alzette sur la carte géologique, depuis sa source à la frontière franco-luxembourgeoise jusqu'à sa confluence dans la Sûre à Ettelbrück, on recoupe pratiquement toutes les couches du Gutland, des plus jeunes vers les plus anciennes, nommées d'après leurs époques de dépôt au sein de l'ère mésozoïque : Dogger, Lias et Trias.

Dans la région des Terres Rouges la rivière traverse la cuesta du Dogger du sud vers le nord, puis elle passe dans les terrains marneux de l'époque du Lias. Dans ces formations tendres les vallées sont larges comme celle du Roeserbann. Au sud de la capitale, l'Alzette rencontre le Grès de Luxembourg, un grès liasique nettement plus résistant. Le petit cours d'eau s'y fraye difficilement un chemin, sinuant dans une vallée en V étroit pour atteindre l'ancienne forteresse de Luxembourg. Par endroits les versants se transforment en parois verticales comme celles du Bock (page 75) avec en contrebas les faubourgs du Grund et de Clausen.

Quittant la capitale en direction du nord, la vallée s'ouvre à nouveau quelque-peu, les falaises s'éloignent du lit qui traverse cette fois les marnes du Trias supérieur tandis que les flancs de vallées plus ou moins écartés sont encore constitués de falaises en grès. À Mersch, l'Alzette laisse la cuesta du Grès de Luxembourg derrière elle pour couler dans un paysage ouvert et vallonné (page 78). Avant de rejoindre la Sûre sur les terrains les plus anciens, ceux du Trias inférieur, l'Alzette traverse le Trias moyen qui comprend des dolomies dures, c'est pourquoi la vallée se resserre au sud d'Ettelbrück.

Les cours d'eau et leurs régions

Les régions naturelles plus petites du Gutland sont souvent caractérisées par l'activité érosive d'un cours d'eau sur un type de roche. La région des Terres rouges constitue une toute petite extension du bassin minier lorrain au sud du pays. Aidée par l'Alzette et la Chiers, l'érosion a dégagé le front de cuesta du Dogger, permettant d'accéder avantageusement par simple galerie au minerai extrait à grande échelle du sous-sol au cours du siècle passé, la couverture au-dessus des couches ferrifères étant par endroits suffisamment faible pour extraire la minette à ciel ouvert. Après la fermeture des mines dans les années soixante-dix, la nature a reconquis ces terrains au point que certains, comme le Prënzebierg, ont été déclarés réserves naturelles.

Une autre région du Gutland, le Müllerthal ou 'Petite Suisse luxembourgeoise', région touristique par excellence, allie un centre de culture et de loisirs, Echternach, avec un arrière-pays calme et riche en sites naturels. L'Ernz Noire, la Sûre et l'Aesbaach ont taillé un relief particulièrement accidenté dans la formation du Grès de Luxembourg qui s'étend de Larochette à Echternach. Les cours d'eau, en creusant leur vallée, dégagent non seulement des falaises aussi hautes que la couche de grès est épaisse, mais finissent par saper la paroi rocheuse qui va bouger. En glissant, celle-ci s'écarte et forme des grottes ou des gorges. Si la paroi bascule et s'écroule, les blocs dégringolent vers les ruisseaux pour y créer un parcours chaotique voire même des petites chutes. En outre, le froid des glaciations et la baisse du niveau de la mer qui s'ensuivit, puis la fonte des glaces empilées lors des périodes froides ainsi que les effets des gel et dégel successifs ont été également des facteurs érosifs importants. En quittant la vallée de l'Ernz Noire, on accède au plateau avec de nombreux points de vue sur les vallées boisées de chênes et de hêtres.

Enfin, la vallée de la Moselle luxembourgeoise est une région viticole par tradition. Le vin y prospère grâce à l'exposition vers le sud-est de ses vignobles plantés sur les marnes du Trias, au climat adouci par les eaux de la Moselle et aux falaises de dolomie qui renvoient la chaleur sur les vignes.

Cette petite histoire géologique montre bien la diversité du sous-sol luxembourgeois. Sur celui-ci se sont mises en place une nature et une culture florissantes que vous allez bientôt découvrir.

Alain Faber
Musée national d'Histoire naturelle, Luxembourg
et Robert Colbach
Service géologique, Luxembourg

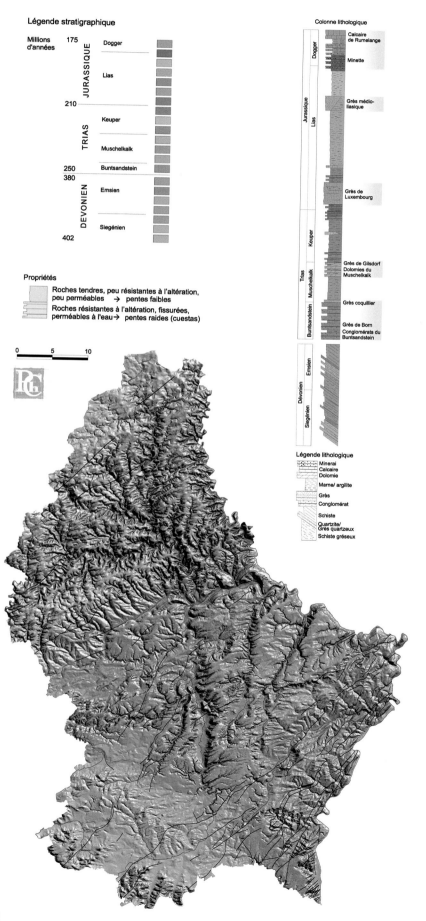

Légende stratigraphique

Millions d'années			
175	JURASSIQUE	Dogger	
		Lias	
210			
	TRIAS	Keuper	
		Muschelkalk	
250		Buntsandstein	
380	DEVONIEN	Emsien	
		Siegénien	
402			

Propriétés

Roches tendres, peu résistantes à l'altération, peu perméables → pentes faibles

Roches résistantes à l'altération, fissurées, perméables à l'eau → pentes raides (cuestas)

0   5   10

Colonne lithologique

Dogger — Calcaire de Rumelange — Minette

Lias — Grès médio-liasique

Jurassique — Grès de Luxembourg

Keuper

Muschelkalk — Grès de Gilsdorf / Dolomies du Muschelkalk

Trias — Grès coquillier

Buntsandstein — Grès de Born / Conglomérats du Buntsandstein

Devonien — Emsien

Siegénien

Légende lithologique
- Minerai
- Calcaire
- Dolomie
- Marne/ argilite
- Grès
- Conglomérat
- Schiste
- Quartzite/ Grès quartzeux
- Schiste gréseux

DAS Großherzogtum Luxemburg teilt nicht nur seine Geschichte sondern auch seine Landschaften mit seinen Nachbarn. So bildet das Gutland – oder *Guttland* im Luxemburgischen – die Verlängerung der Gaume nach Osten und die der Lorraine nach Norden hin. Ebenso setzt das Ösling oder *Éislek* die Ardennen nach Osten und die Eifel nach Westen fort. Die beiden natürlichen Regionen – das Gutland im Süden und das Ösling im Norden – unterscheiden sich in verschiedener Hinsicht deutlich voneinander, zum Beispiel durch das Gestein, aus dem der Untergrund besteht, die Form der Täler, die von den Flüssen gebildet wurden, die Flora und Fauna, die sich hier entfaltet haben, und die Lebensweise der Einwohner.

Eine Linie, die Roodt mit Fouhren verbindet, trennt diese Regionen mit ihren sehr unterschiedlichen geologischen Untergründen: Im Norden ein Grundgebirge aus dem Paläozoikum (vor 540 bis 240 Millionen Jahren) und im Süden das Deckgebirge aus dem Mesozoikum (vor 250 bis 65 Millionen Jahren). Ebenso wie das Rheinische Schiefergebirge gehört das Ösling zu der Gebirgskette, deren Reste sich von den französischen Ardennen bis zum Rhein erstrecken. Das Gutland bildet den nord-östlichen Ausläufer des Pariser Beckens, die Luxemburger Bucht.

Das Gestein des Öslings entstand vor rund 390 bis 380 Millionen Jahren aus den Ablagerungen von Lehm- und Sandschichten auf dem Grund eines Meeres. Die Geologen bezeichnen diese Zeit als Unterdevon. Vor etwa 350 Millionen Jahren wurden die Schichten dieses Ablagerungsgesteins dann während der herzynischen Gebirgsbildung, bei der die Sedimente zu Dachschiefer, Schiefer, Sandstein, Quarzophylladen und Quarzit umgewandelt wurden, hoch gefaltet, wobei hohe Gipfel empor ragten. Dann verschwand die durch die Erosion abgetragene junge Gebirgskette nach und nach und hinterließ nur eine weite Rumpfebene mit flachen Erhebungen, die sich fast auf Meerhöhe erstreckte.

Vor 225 Millionen Jahren wurde diese Erosionsfläche des devonischen Gebirges erneut vom Meer überschwemmt. Das Meer dehnte sich von Osten nach Westen hin aus, um sich später nach Süden und Südwesten hin zu öffnen und eine weite Meeresfläche zu bilden, deren Mittelpunkt das Pariser Becken war. Der paläozoische Untergrund wurde dann zu einem großen Teil von Ablagerungen des frühen Mesozoikums überdeckt. Gegen Ende des Mesozoikums zog sich das Meer endgültig aus unseren Regionen zurück. Anschließend wurde die Landschaft durch Erosion und die Hebung des Öslings, die rascher und stärker als die des Gutlandes ausfiel, umgestaltet.

Von der Obersauer bis zur Our

Die heutige Landschaft des Öslings wird durch eine Ebene geprägt, die eine Höhe von ungefähr 500 m aufweist. Diese Hochebene, die im Nordwesten sehr weitflächig und weithin von Weideland und Feldern bedeckt ist, verliert ihre Ausdehnung zum Süden und Südosten hin, wo sie von den engen Tälern der Sauer, des Unterlaufs der Our und ihrer Zuflüsse stark zerklüftet wird. Die Höhenunterschiede von den engen Talböden bis zu den Hochflächen betragen häufig über 100 m: In Vianden liegt das in 300 m Höhe auf einem Felsvorsprung zu findende Schloss rund 100 Meter über der Our (siehe weiter unten S. 136-137), während das ganz in der Nähe befindliche Wasserbecken des Pumpspeicherkraft-werkes in 500 m Höhe auf dem Gipfel des Nikolausberges angelegt wurde. Die steilen Hänge sind bewaldet. Das Holz wird genutzt, wobei die Eichen, deren Rinde früher zum Gerben von Leder genutzt wurde, heute häufig Nadelhölzern Platz gemacht haben.

Das Flussnetz des Öslings besteht vor allem aus der Sauer und ihren nördlichen Zuflüssen. Dazu gehört unter anderem auch die Clerf. Sie fließt von Norden nach Süden und durchquert die drei großen von Südwesten nach Nordosten verlaufenden Gebirgsfaltungen: den Sattel von Bastogne, die Mulde von Wiltz und den Sattel von Givonne.

Talabwärts von Clerf durchquert der gleichnamige Bach Sandsteine und Quarzophylladen, härteres und älteres Gestein, das an der Südflanke einer großen Faltung in Form eines Sattels, des sogenannten Sattels von Bastogne ansteht. Weiter südlich schließt sich eine Faltung in Form einer Regenrinne, die Mulde von Wiltz an, die von weicheren Schiefern gebildet wird, welche eine leichte Senkung mit weniger hügeligem Relief bilden. Zwischen Drauffelt und Lellingen ist das Clerftal nicht so eng, und die Talhänge sind flacher. Danach trifft der Bach auf die härteren Schichten der Nordflanke des Sattels von Givonne, und bis Göbelsmühle sind die Täler wieder besonders eng.

Die Ausrichtung der Mäander der Flüsse des Öslings folgt häufig der Richtung der geologischen Schichten und der zahlreichen Verwerfungen und Klüfte. Die frei liegenden Felsvorsprünge bieten eine günstige Lage für Burgen wie Clerf, Esch/Sauer, Bourscheid und Vianden.

Die Schichtstufenlandschaft

Ein Schnitt in den Untergrund zeigt uns, dass das im Ösling anstehende devonische Grundgebirge sich nach Süden fortsetzt, wo es jedoch durch jüngere Schichten des Gutlandes überlagert wird. Diese mesozoische Deckschicht des nördlichen Gutlandes beginnt in der unteren Trias vor rund 225 Millionen Jahren mit Sandschein- bzw. Konglomeratschichten. Nach Südwesten hin stehen immer jüngere Deckschichten an, von denen die letzten die vor 175 Millionen Jahren abgelagerten Doggerkalke nahe der französischen Grenze sind.

In diesem nahezu horizontalen Schichtenpaket, das zum Zentrum des Pariser Beckens hin leicht einfällt, wechseln hartes Gestein – Sandstein, Kalkstein, Dolomit... – mit weicherem Gestein, überwiegend Mergel ab. Dieser Wechsel führte zur Schichtstufenlandschaft, die sich durch unterschiedlich starke Erosion der verschiedenen Schichten im Laufe der letzten Millionen Jahren ausgebildet hat: Die harten Schichten bilden den Stirnhang der Schichtstufen-landschaft mit starker Neigung, während die weicheren überlagernden Schichten den Flachhang bilden. Am stärksten ausgeprägt sind die Schichtstufe des Luxemburger Sandsteins aus dem unteren Lias und die Dogger-Stufe.

Nördlich der Schichtstufe des Luxemburger Sandsteins, die sich zwischen Beckerich, Mersch und Nommern erstreckt, wird das mergelige Vorland für die Landwirtschaft genutzt, während der Sandstein-Stirnhang von Laubwäldern bestanden ist. In Nommern liegt das Dorf im mergeligen Vorland, während die Nommerlayen (Seite 92) den Standstein-Stirnhang darstellen, und die leicht nach Süden hin geneigte Ebene den von jüngerem Mergel bedeckten Cuesta-Flachhang bildet.

Die Doggerstufe, die in Lothringen durch die Moselhöhe verlängert wird, ist eine doppelte Schichtstufe. Sie wird von zwei widerstandsfähigen Schichten, der Minette und den Doggerkalken, gebildet, die durch eine geringmächtige weichere Schicht getrennt sind. Der Prënzebierg mit seinem ehemaligen Tagebau (Seite 45 bis 47) sowie der Tëtelbierg, der durch seine Treverer-Stadt (Seite 24) gekrönt wird, gehören zur Doggerstufe. Sie reichen ein wenig weiter ins Vorland hinein, da die Erosion dort etwas weniger rasch erfolgt ist.

Die drei Hügel, die dem Cuesta-Stirnhang in der Nähe von

Differdingen vorgelagert sind, Zolverknapp (422 Meter), Loetschet und Packebierg, bilden die Wasserscheide zwischen den Becken der Mosel (Alzette) und der Maas (Korn). Die Korn fließt am Fuße der Cuesta entlang und verlässt Luxemburg nach Westen. Sie ist der einzige luxemburgische Wasserlauf, der zur Maas fließt. Alle anderen fließen direkt oder indirekt in die Mosel.

Die Alzette von Süden nach Norden

Folgt man der Alzette auf der geologischen Karte von ihrer Quelle an der französisch-luxemburgischen Grenze bis zu ihrem Zusammenfluss mit der Sauer bei Ettelbrück, so durchquert man fast alle Schichten des Gutlandes, von den jüngeren zu den älteren, die nach ihren Ablagerungs-Epochen innerhalb des mesozoischen Zeitalters Dogger, Lias und Trias genannt werden.

In der Minette-Gegend durchfließt der Fluss die Doggerstufe von Süden nach Norden, um dann in die Mergel des Lias zu gelangen. In diesen weichen Formationen sind die Täler, wie zum Beispiel die Talebene des Roserbannes, weit.

Südlich der Hauptstadt trifft die Alzette auf den Luxemburger Sandstein, einen wesentlich widerstands-fähigeren Lias-Sandstein. Der kleine Wasserlauf gräbt sich dort mühevoll seinen Weg durch ein enges V-Tal, um die ehemalige Festung Luxemburg zu erreichen. Hier sind die Talhänge, wie die des Bockfelsens (Seite 75) entlang der Vororte Grund und Clausen, stellenweise senkrecht.

Nördlich der Hauptstadt verbreitert sich das Tal wieder ein wenig, die Felswände entfernen sich vom Flussbett, das hier in den Mergeln der oberen Trias liegt, während die mehr oder weniger weit auseinander liegenden Hänge der Täler noch aus Sandsteinfelsen bestehen. In Mersch verlässt die Alzette den Luxemburger Sandstein und tritt in eine offene und gewellte Landschaft ein (Seite 78). Bevor sie auf den ältesten Bereichen, denen der unteren Trias, in die Sauer mündet, durchquert die Alzette die der mittleren Trias, die teilweise aus harten Dolomitsteinen bestehen und das Tal südlich von Ettelbrück wieder einengen.

Die Flussläufe und ihre Regionen

Die kleineren Naturgebiete des Gutlandes sind meistens von der Abtragung einer bestimmten Gesteinsschicht durch einen Wasserlauf geprägt. Die *Minette*-Gegend stellt einen kleinen Ausläufer des lothringischen Kohlebeckens südlich des Landes dar. Mit Hilfe von Alzette und Korn hat die Erosion die Doggerstufe freigelegt, so dass es möglich wurde, über einen einfachen Stollen leicht an das Erz – das im Laufe des vergangenen Jahrhunderts in großem Stile aus dem Untergrund abgebaut worden war – zu gelangen, da die Decke über den erzführenden Schichten stellenweise so dünn war, dass die *Minette* im Tagebau gefördert werden konnte. Nach Schließung der Bergwerke in den siebziger Jahren hat die Natur diese Gebiete wieder zurückerobert, und zwar in der Weise, dass einige wie der Prënzebierg zu Naturschutzgebieten erklärt wurden.

Eine andere Region des Gutlands, das Müllerthal oder die ‚Kleine Luxemburger Schweiz', eine Fremdenverkehrsregion par excellence, verbindet ein Kultur- und Freizeitzentrum Echternach mit einem ruhigen Hinterland, das reich an Naturlandschaften ist. Die Schwarze Ernz, die Sauer und der Aesbaach haben im Luxemburger Sandstein, der sich von Larochette bis Echternach erstreckt, ein gebirgsähnliches Relief gebildet. Wenn die Wasserläufe ihr Tal graben, legen sie nicht nur Felsen frei, deren Höhe der Stärke der Sandsteinschicht entspricht, sondern unterspülen auch die Felswand, die schließlich in Bewegung gerät. Sie rutscht ab, teilt sich und bildet Höhlen oder Schluchten. Wenn die Wand umkippt und einstürzt, fallen die Blöcke in die Bäche, um dort einen chaotischen Lauf oder sogar kleine Wasserfälle zu bilden. Auch die Kälte der Vereisungen und das darauf folgende Absinken des Meeresspiegels, dann das Schmelzen des während der Kältezeiten aufgeschichteten Eises sowie die Auswirkungen des aufeinander folgenden Gefrierens und Auftauens waren wesentliche Faktoren für die Erosion. Wenn man die Schwarze Ernz verlässt, gelangt man zur Hochebene, die zahlreiche Aussichtspunkte auf die mit Eichen und Buchen bestandenen Täler aufweist.

Schließlich ist das luxemburgische Moseltal ein traditionelles Weinbaugebiet. Dank der südöstlichen Ausrichtung der auf den Mergeln des Trias gepflanzten Weinberge, des durch das Wasser der Mosel abgemilderten Klimas und der Dolomitfelswände, die die Sonnenwärme auf die Weinberge reflektieren, gedeiht der Wein hier sehr gut.

Dieser kleine geologische Exkurs zeigt die Vielfalt der Luxemburger Gesteinsformationen, auf denen eine blühende Natur und Kultur entstand, die Sie nun auf den Bildern entdecken werden.

Alain Faber
Nationales Naturgeschichtliches Museum, Luxemburg
und Robert Colbach
Geologisches Landesamt, Luxemburg

THE Grand Duchy of Luxembourg shares not only its history but also its physical characteristics with its neighbours. The Gutland (Good Land), or *Guttland* in the Luxembourg language, is the eastern extension of the Gaume in Belgium and the northern part of the Lorraine in France. In the same way the Oesling or *Eislek* is part of the ancient mountain range known as the Ardennes in the west and as the Eifel in the east. The division between these two natural regions – the Gutland in the south and the Oesling in the north – is clearly defined in several ways: the rocks forming the subsoil, the shape of the valleys carved out by the rivers, the flora and fauna native to each region and the lifestyle of the inhabitants.

A line running from Roodt to Fouhren delimits these regions of differing rock substrata. In the northern section the bedrock dates from the Palaeozoic era of some 540 to 250 million years ago. In the southern region the overlying beds date from the Mesozoic period of 250 to 65 million years ago. The Oesling, like the Middle Rhine Highlands, is part of an eroded chain of mountains stretching from the French Ardennes to the Rhine. The Gutland, on the other hand, forms the Gulf of Luxembourg on the extreme northeast of the Paris Basin.

The rock of the Oesling was formed some 390 to 380 million years ago by deposits of mud and sand on the seabed. Geologists call this epoch the Lower Devonian. These strata of sedimentary rocks were later folded during the *Hercynian orogeny* about 350 million years ago when the sediments turned into slate, schist, quartz sandstone, quartzophyllites and quartzites during the mountain building period. Little by little the young mountain chain was eroded, leaving only a huge peneplain of low altitude, nearly at sea level.

This erosion surface of the Devonian massif was once more covered by the sea some 225 million years ago which progressed steadily from east to west, and later to the south and southwest, forming a vast sea, the centre of which was the Paris Basin. The Palaeozoic bedrock was thus mostly covered by deposits of the early Mesozoic. Towards the end of the Mesozoic the sea withdrew completely from our region. The landscape was later transformed by erosion and by lifting, more rapid and more extensive in the Oesling than in the Gutland.

From the Haute Sûre to the Our

The present day landscape of the Oesling is that of a tableland of more or less 500 meters of altitude. This high plateau, very extensive in the northwest and mostly covered with fields and pastures, diminishes in size to the south and southeast where the steep valleys of the Sûre, the lower Our and their tributaries divide it. The difference in height between the bottoms of the narrow valleys and the sloping shoulders is often more than one hundred meters, such as at Vianden where the castle perched on a rocky spur of 300 meters altitude dominates the Our below (pages 136-137) while the nearby reservoir of the power plant is situated at 500 meters on the summit of Mount Saint Nicholas. The abrupt slopes are covered by forests of conifers, often replacing the thickets of oaks of which the bark was used for tanning in the leather industry.

The river system of the Oesling is formed mainly by the Sûre and its northern tributaries. The Clerve, in particular, during its course from north to south crosses the three large folds that cross the region from the southwest to the northeast: the anticline of Bastogne, the Syncline of Wiltz and the anticline of Givonne.

Downstream from Clervaux the Clerve flows through outcrops of sandstone and quartzophillites, harder and older rocks, found on the south slope of the anticline of Bastogne, a large, saddle-shaped fold. It is followed farther to the south is the gutter-shaped fold of the Wiltz syncline consisting of softer schist in a shallow trough of smoother contours. Thus, from Drauffelt to Lellingen the Clerve valley is less narrow and the slopes less steep. Finally the river arrives at the harder formations of the north slope of the Givonne anticline and, until Goebelsmühle, the valleys are once more very narrow and deep.

The meanders of the rivers of the Oesling mostly follow the direction of the geological layers and the many faults and joints. Prominent rocky spurs offer superb emplacements for castles such as Clervaux, Esch-sur-Sûre, Bourscheid and Vianden, among others.

The Cuesta Countryside

A sample of the subsoil demonstrates that the Devonian bedrock, near the surface in the Oesling, continues southerly where it is covered, however, by the younger formations of the Gutland. This Mesozoic overburden in the north of the Gutland dates from the Lower Triassic of about 225 million years ago and consists of layers of sandstone and conglomerate rock. Farther to the southwest younger layers are superposed, the last being the Dogger limestone of the Jurassic, deposited 175 million years ago, found near the French border.

In this mass of nearly horizontal layers, descending several degrees toward the centre of the Paris Basin, are alternating layers of harder rocks such as sandstone, limestone and dolomites and more friable rock, particularly marl. This alternation is the origin of the *cuestas* or homoclinal ridges formed by the more or less rapid erosion of the different rock layers during the last few millions of years. The harder rock forms the front slope of the cuesta in a steep cliff or escarpment while the softer rock forms the gentle dip or back slope. The most prominent cuestas are those of the Luxembourg sandstone, dating from the Lower Lias and the Dogger

To the north of the front slope of the Luxembourg Sandstone, stretching between Beckerich, Mersch and Nommern, the marl foreland is devoted to agriculture whereas deciduous forests cover the sandstone scarp. At Nommern the village is in the marl foreland while the Nommerlayen (page 92) make up the sandstone escarpment. The tableland inclines slightly towards the south, forming the back slope of the cuesta, covered with marl of more recent origin.

The cuesta of the Dogger period, extended by the Moselle incline in Lorraine, has a double front slope formed by two layers of resistant rock, the *Minette* and the Dogger limestone, separated by a softer, shallow formation. The Prënzenbierg with its open pit mine (pages 45 to 47) as well as the Tëtelbierg crowned by its Trevire oppidum (page 24) are found in the Dogger cuesta. The double fronts extend a little farther into the foreland for the erosion was less rapid in this region.

The three hills preceding the front slopes of the cuesta near Differdange are the Zolverknapp at 422 meters, the Loetschet and the Packebierg. They form the watershed of the Moselle basin, that is, the course of the Alzette and the basin of the Meuse to which the Chiers flows. This river runs along the base of the cuesta, flowing west. It is the only Luxembourg river that feeds the Meuse, as the others all join, sooner or later, the Moselle.

The Alzette, from south to north

While following the course of the Alzette on the geological map, from its source at the Franco-Luxembourg frontier to its confluence with the Sûre at Ettelbrück, one covers nearly all the layers of Gutland, from the youngest to the oldest, named after the periods when they were deposited during the Mesozoic, namely the Dogger, the Lias and the Triassic.

In the Red Earth region the river crosses the Dogger cuesta from south to north and then passes through the marl deposits of the Lias period. In these soft formations the valleys are wide, such as at Roeserbann. South of the capital the Alzette meets the Luxembourg Sandstone, a sandstone of the Lias era which is far more resistant. The little river flows with difficulty through this terrain, winding through a narrow V-shaped valley to reach the ancient stronghold of Luxembourg. In some areas the valley slopes become vertical walls, such as those of Bock (page 75) facing the suburbs of Grund and Clausen.

Heading north from the capital the valley opens up slightly once more and the cliffs recede from the riverbed that now crosses the marl of the Upper Triassic. Sandstone still forms the cliffs of these slightly wider valleys. The Alzette leaves the Luxembourg Sandstone cuesta at Mersch, now flowing through open, undulating countryside (page 78). Before joining the Sûre on the older terrain of the Lower Triassic the Alzette crosses the Middle Triassic region of hard dolomite rock; this is why the valley narrows south of Ettelbrück.

The rivers and their regions

The smallest natural regions of Gutland are often defined by the erosion of certain types of rock by water. The Red Earth region is a small extension of the Lorraine mining basin in the south of the country. Erosion, aided by the Alzette and the Chiers, had cleared the front slope of the Dogger cuesta, making it easy in the last century to extract ore on a large scale. The overburden above the iron bearing layers was so shallow that in some places the *minette* could be mined by open pit methods. After the closure of the mines in the 'seventies nature took over the terrain to such a degree that some, as at Prënzebierg, are now protected nature reserves.

Another region of the Gutland, the Müllerthal or the 'Little Switzerland of Luxembourg' is a noted tourist destination, with its cultural and leisure centre of Echternach and its tranquil hinterland with many beautiful natural sites. The Black Ernz, the Sûre and Aesbaach have carved out a particularly irregular relief in the Luxembourg Sandstone formation that runs from Larochette to Echternach. The rivers while carving out their valleys have created cliffs as high as the layer of sandstone is deep but also undermine the rocky walls that will eventually shift. When this happens they diverge, creating caves or gorges. If the rock face tumbles, huge blocks of stone slide down towards the streams, forming chaotic riverbeds and even small waterfalls. The cold of the Ice Age and the lowering of the sea level that followed as well as the melting of the glaciers in the frigid eras combined with the following eras of freezing and thawing were also important factors in the erosive process. When leaving the valley of the Black Ernz one arrives at a plateau with numerous viewpoints on the wooded valleys of oak and beech.

Finally there is the valley of the Luxembourg Moselle, traditionally a wine-growing region. The vineyards, planted on the southeast facing slopes of Triassic marl, with a climate softened by the waters of the Moselle and radiant heat produced by the dolomite cliffs, are extremely productive.

This little geological history illustrates the diversity of the subsoil of Luxembourg on which both nature and a flourishing culture that you will soon discover is based.

Alain Faber
Natural History Museum of Luxembourg
and Robert Colbach,
Geological Service of Luxembourg

HET Groothertdogdom Luxemburg deelt niet alleen zijn geschiedenis, maar ook zijn landschappen met zijn buren. Het Gutland, of *Guttland* in het Luxemburgs, vormt aan de oostkant het verlengstuk van de Gaume en in het noorden van de Lorraine. Zo zet de Oesling, of *Éislek*, ook de Ardennen in oostelijke richting en de Eifel in Westelijke richting voort. Deze twee natuurlijke gebieden – het Gutland in het zuiden en de Oesling in het noorden – onderscheiden zich in meerdere opzichten duidelijk van elkaar: bijvoorbeeld door de rotsachtige ondergrond, de door rivieren uitgeholde valleien, de fauna en flora die zich hier ontwikkeld hebben, de levenswijze van hun inwoners…

Een lijn die Roodt met Fouhren verbindt, scheidt deze gebieden met hun sterk uiteenlopende geologische ondergronden. In het noordelijk gedeelte een grondgebergte dat dateert uit het Paleozoïcum (d.w.z. van 540 tot 250 miljoen jaar geleden) en in het zuidelijk gedeelte dekgesteente dat dateert uit het Mesozoïcum (van 250 tot 65 miljoen jaar geleden). De Oesling maakt, net zoals het Rijns leisteengebergte, deel uit van de bergketen waarvan de resten zich van de Franse Ardennen tot de Rijn uitstrekken. Het Gutland vormt de Baai van Luxemburg en vormt de noordoostelijke uitloper van het bekken van Parijs.

De rotsen van de Oesling ontstonden zo'n 390 tot 380 miljoen jaar geleden uit de afzettingen van leem- en zandlagen op de zeebodem. De geologen noemen dit tijdperk het Onder-Devoon. Ongeveer 350 miljoen jaar geleden werden deze sedimentaire rotslagen dan in de loop van de hercynische gebergtevorming geplooid. Daarbij werden de sedimenten omgezet in leisteen, schalies, kwartszandsteen, kwartsfylladen en kwartsiet, terwijl zich hoge toppen vormden. Vervolgens erodeerde de jonge bergketen. Hij verdween beetje bij beetje en liet slechts een grote schiervlakte achter met lage verhevenheden die zich bijna op het niveau van de zeespiegel bevond.

225 miljoen geleden werd deze erosievallei van het devonisch gebergte opnieuw door de zee overstroomd. Deze strekte zich van het oosten tot het westen uit, om zich later een weg te banen naar het zuiden en het zuidwesten om daar een breed zeeoppervlak te vormen waarvan het middelpunt het bekken van Parijs was. De palezoïsche steenlaag werd toen grotendeels bedekt met afzettingen uit het vroege Mesozoïcum. Tegen het einde van het Mesozoïcum trok de zee zich definitief uit onze gebieden terug. Het landschap werd vervolgens geremodelleerd door de erosie en de heffing van de Oesling die sneller en sterker verliep dan die van het Gutland.

Van de Boven-Sûre tot de Our

Het huidig landschap van de Oesling wordt gekenmerkt door een plateau dat een hoogte heeft van ongeveer 500 meter. Deze hoogvlakte is zeer uitgestrekt in het noordwesten en is verregaand bedekt met weilanden en velden. Ze moet wat van haar uitgestrektheid inboeten naar het zuiden en het zuidwesten toe, waar ze sterk versneden wordt door de smalle valleien van de Sûre, de benedenloop van de Our en hun zijrivieren. De hoogteverschillen tussen de smalle dalbodems en de hoogvlakten bedragen vaak meer dan honderd meter. In Vianden staat het kasteel verheven op een uitstekende rots op een hoogte van 300 m en ligt daarmee zo'n 100 meter hoger dan de Our (zie de pagina's 136 -137 hierna), terwijl het waterbekken van de nabij gelegen elektrische

centrale aangelegd werd op een hoogte van 500 meter op de top van de Sint-Niklaasberg. De steile hellingen zijn bebost. Het hout wordt geëxploiteerd. De eiken, waarvan de schors vroeger vaak gebruikt werd voor het leerlooien, hebben tegenwoordig vaak plaats geruimd voor naaldbomen.

Het riviernetwerk van de Oesling bestaat voornamelijk uit de Sûre en zijn noordelijke bijrivieren. De Clerve stroomt van het noorden naar het zuiden en doorkruist de drie grote plooien die van het zuidwesten naar het noordoosten door het gebied lopen: het zadel of de anticlinale van Bastenaken, de synclinale van Wiltz en de anticlinale van Givonne.

Dalafwaarts van Clervaux doorkruist de Clerve de zandsteen en de kwartsfylladen, hardere en oudere rotsen die tevoorschijn komen op de zuidflank van een grote plooi in de vorm van een zadel: het zadel of de anticlinale van Bastenaken. Verder naar het zuiden wordt deze opgevolgd door een plooi in de vorm van een regengoot, de synclinale van Wiltz die bestaat uit zachtere schisten en een lichte depressie vormt met een heuvelachtig reliëf. Van Drauffelt tot Lellingen is de vallei van de Clerve minder smal en zijn de hellingen minder steil. Tot slot stoot de rivier op de hardere formaties van de noordflank van de anticlinale van Givonne en tot in Goebelsmühle zijn de valleien opnieuw bijzonder smal.

De richting van de meanders van de rivieren van de Oesling volgt vaak de richting van de geologische lagen en van de talrijke verschuivingen en kloven. De vrijliggende uitspringende rotsen bieden een bevoorrechte plaats voor kastelen zoals dat van Clervaux, Esch-sur-Sûre, Bourscheid en Vianden.

Het cuestalandschap

Een snede in de ondergrond toont ons dat het devonisch grondgebergte in de Oesling naar het zuiden voortgezet wordt, waar dit evenwel bedekt wordt door de jongere formaties van het Gutland. Deze mesozoïsche deklaag in het noorden van Gutland begint in de onderste Trias ongeveer 225 miljoen jaar geleden, met zanderige lagen en zelfs conglomeraatlagen. Naar het zuiden toe ontstaan steeds jongere deklagen, waarvan de laatste de kalksteenlagen van de Dogger zijn die daar meer dan 175 miljoen jaar geleden nabij de Franse grens afgezet werden.

In dit nagenoeg horizontale lagenpakket, dat naar het centrum van het bekken van Parijs toe lichtjes invalt, wisselen het hard gesteente (zandsteen, kalksteen, dolomiet…) en het zacht gesteente (overwegend mergel) elkaar af. Deze afwisseling ligt aan de oorsprong van het cuesta-landschap. Dit ontstond door de uiteenlopende snelheid van de erosie van de diverse lagen in de loop van de laatste miljoenen jaren: de harde rotslaag vormt het front van de cuesta, met een steile helling en de zachtere formatie bedekt de zacht glooiende rugzijde. De twee meest uitgesproken cuesta's zijn deze van de Zandsteen van Luxemburg, die dateert uit de Onder-Lias en die van de Dogger.

Ten noorden van het front van de cuesta van de Luxemburgse zandsteen, die zich uitstrekt tussen Beckerich, Mersch en Nommern, wordt het mergelhoudend voorland voor de landbouw gebruikt, terwijl het zanderig front begroeid wordt met loofbossen. In Nommern bevindt het dorp zich in het mergelhoudend voorland, terwijl de Nommerlayen (pagina 92) het zanderig front vormen. Het plateau verloopt lichtjes hellend naar het zuiden en vormt de rugzijde van de cuesta die bedekt is met jongere mergel.

De cuesta van de Dogger, die in Lotharingen door de Moezelhelling verlengd wordt, heeft een dubbel front dat bestaat uit twee harde lagen, de Minette en de kalksteen van de Dogger, die van elkaar gescheiden worden door een zachtere en dunnere formatie. De Prënzebierg met zijn voormalige open groeve (pagina's 45 tot 47) en de Tëtelbierg die met zijn *oppidum trevira* ("Treverer Stadt") bekroond wordt (pagina 24) maken deel uit van de cuesta van de Dogger. Ze reiken wat verderop tot in het voorland, want daar is de erosie wat minder snel verlopen.

De drie heuvels die het front van de cuesta nabij Differdange voorafgaan, de Zolverknapp (422 meter), de Loetschet en de Packebierg, vormen samen de waterscheiding tussen de bekkens van de Moezel, d.w.z. de Alzette, en de Maas, de Chiers. Deze vloeit aan de voet van de cuesta en verlaat Luxemburg naar het westen. Hij is de enige waterloop die in de Maas uitmondt. Alle anderen vervoegen vroeg of laat de Moezel.

De Alzette van zuid tot noord

Als we het parcours van de Alzette op de geologische kaart volgen vanaf zijn oorsprong aan de Frans-Luxemburgse grens tot hij in Ettelbrück samenvloeit met de Sûre, dan ziet men dat deze door bijna alle lagen van het Gutland stroomt, van de jongste tot de oudste, en die genoemd zijn naar de tijdperken van hun afzetting binnen de mesozoïsche era: Dogger, Lias en Trias.

In het gebied van *Terres Rouges*, de Minette-streek, doorkruist de rivier de cuesta van de Dogger van het zuiden naar het noorden en loopt vervolgens in de mergelachtige terreinen van de Lias. In deze zachte formaties zijn de valleien breed, zoals deze van de Roeserbann. Ten zuiden van de hoofdstad stoot de Alzette terug op de Luxemburgse zandsteen, een zandsteen uit de Lias met een aanzienlijk hogere weerstand. De kleine waterloop kan zich daar maar moeilijk een weg banen en loopt kronkelend door een smal V-dal om de voormalige vesting van Luxemburg te bereiken. Op sommige plaatsen zijn de hellingen loodrechte wanden, zoals die van de Bock (pagina 75) langsheen de voorsteden van Grund en Clausen.

Ten Noorden van de hoofdstad wordt de vallei terug wat breder. De rotswanden verwijderen zich van de rivierbedding die hier in de mergel van de Boven-Trias ligt, terwijl de min of meer uiteenstaande flanken nog uit zandsteenrotsen bestaan.

In Mersch laat de Alzette de cuesta van de Luxemburgse zandsteen achter zich om in een open en glooiend landschap te vloeien (pagina 78). Voordat hij de Sûre op de oudste terreinen vervoegt, namelijk die van de Beneden-Trias, steekt de Alzette de Midden-Trias over die gedeeltelijk uit harde dolomieten bestaat. Daardoor wordt de vallei ten zuiden van Ettelbrück terug wat smaller.

De waterlopen en hun gebieden

De kleinere natuurgebieden van het Gutland worden vaak gekenmerkt door de erosie van een bepaald rotstype door een waterloop. Het gebied van *Terres rouges* vormt een kleine uitloper van het steenkoolbekken van Lotharingen in het zuiden van het land. Geholpen door de Alzette en de Chiers heeft de erosie het front van de cuesta van de Dogger vrijgelegd, zodat het mogelijk werd om via een eenvoudige gang gemakkelijk bij het erts te komen, dat in de loop van de vorige eeuw op grote schaal uit de ondergrond ontgonnen werd. De deklagen boven de ertslagen waren op sommige plaatsen zo dun dat het erts in dagbouw ontgonnen kon worden. Bij de sluiting van de mijnen in de jaren zeventig, heeft de natuur deze terreinen terug veroverd en weliswaar zodanig dat sommige ervan, zoals de Prënzebierg tot natuurreservaat uitgeroepen werden.

Een ander gebied van het Gutland, het Müllerthal of 'Klein Luxemburgs Zwitserland', een toeristisch gebied bij uitstek, verbindt het cultuur- en vrijetijdscentrum Echternach met een rustig achterland dat rijk is aan natuurgebieden. De Zwarte Ernz, de Sûre en de Aesbaach hebben in de Luxemburgse zandsteen die zich van Larochette tot Echternach uitstrekt, voor een bergachtig reliëf gezorgd. Door de uitholling van hun vallei hebben de waterlopen niet alleen de rotsen vrijgelegd, waarvan de hoogte overeenkomt met de weerstand van hun zandsteenlagen, maar hebben ze ook de rotswand ondergraven die daardoor gaat bewegen. De rotswand glijdt weg, splitst zich en vormt grotten of spelonken. Als de wand omvalt en instort, rollen de blokken in het water om daar een chaotisch parcours, of zelfs kleine watervalletjes te creëren. Ook de koude van de ijstijd, de daarop volgende daling van de zeespiegel en vervolgens de smelting van de ijslagen die zich tijdens de ijstijd opgestapeld hadden, alsook de opeenvolgende effecten van het bevriezen en het ontdooien vormden belangrijke factoren voor de erosie. Bij het verlaten van de vallei van de Zwarte Ernz, komt men op het plateau met talrijke uitkijkpunten op de valleien die bebost zijn met eiken en beuken.

Tot slot is de Luxemburgse Moezelvallei een wijnbouwgebied bij uitstek. De wijnbouw gedijt er goed doordat de wijngaarden, die op de mergelgrond van de Trias geplant zijn, zuidoost gericht zijn. Het klimaat in het Moezeldal is bijzonder zacht en de rotswanden van de dolomieten weerkaatsen de warmte van de zon op de druiven.

Deze beknopte geologische geschiedenis toont de verscheidenheid van de Luxemburgse ondergrond waarop een bloeiende natuur en cultuur ontstaan is waarmee u nu kunt kennismaken.

Alain Faber,
Nationaal Museum van Natuurwetenschappen,
Luxemburg
en Robert Colbach,
Geologische Dienst, Luxemburg

Au cœur de l'histoire européenne
Im Herzen der europäischen Geschichte
In the Heart of the European History
In het hart van de Europese geschiedenis

L'empreinte de Rome

TOUT concourrait à faciliter la pénétration de la civilisation romaine dans le Luxembourg. Deux grandes chaussées reliaient Trèves, l'une à Lyon, l'autre à Reims. Une troisième se dirigeait vers Cologne. Toute proche du futur Luxembourg, Trèves, fondée par l'empereur Auguste en 15 avant Jésus-Christ, était considérée comme «la seconde Rome»; à partir de 295 et durant tout le IVe siècle les empereurs y séjournèrent souvent.

L'agriculture, l'élevage et les métiers auxquels s'adonnaient les Celtes attirèrent les militaires et administrateurs romains de Metz autant que de Trèves. De confortables villae furent construites par des notables et de riches commerçants. Les ruines de l'une des plus sompteuses furent découvertes en 1975 à Schwaarz-uecht près d'Echter-nach (page de droite), et en 1995 furent mis à jour dans les vestiges d'une villa à Vichten une splendide mosaïque représentant les neuf muses entourant le poète Homère (double page suivante).

D'autres mosaïques provenant de villae gallo-romaines furent découvertes à Diekirch. À Mamer, vicus situé sur la chaussée de Trèves à Reims, des thermes publics dotés d'un hypocauste et de nombreuses sculptures ont été dégagés lors des fouilles. À Steinsel, en pleine forêt, se dressait un temple gallo-romain entouré de plusieurs bâtiments du Ier au IVe siècle. De la grande villa de Mersch au confluent de l'Alzette et de l'Eisch subsistent l'hypocauste et une partie de l'immense bassin de 75 mètres de longueur.

Les fouilles dans les ruines de la villa agricole de Koerich (double page précédente) ont révélé l'existence, au Ier siècle, d'un vaste ensemble de constructions entouré d'un rempart. Au Tëtelbierg près de Rodange, les vestiges de l'oppidum celtique (ci-dessus) de près de trois kilomètres de circonférence datent du Ier siècle avant Jésus-Christ. L'ouvrage défensif fut occupé ensuite par les Romains. À tous ces vestiges s'ajoutent les autels votifs tel celui visible en l'église de Berdorf (pages 28 à 37), les monuments funéraires, les stèles sculptées, les statues de divinités, les objets de la vie quotidienne et les monnaies à l'effigie de différents empereurs.

À la faveur de la pax romana, le christianisme s'introduisit dans le pays en même temps que la culture de la vigne.

En 395 la préfecture des Gaules quitta Trèves pour Arles. C'était la fin de l'emprise romaine sur le territoire.

Die Spuren von Rom

ES waren alle Voraussetzungen vorhanden, die Verbreitung der römischen Zivilisation in Luxemburg zu erleichtern. Zwei große Straßen verbanden Trier mit Lyon bzw. Reims. Eine dritte führte nach Köln. Das von Kaiser Augustus im Jahre 15 vor Christus gegründete, ganz in der Nähe des künftigen Luxemburgs gelegene Trier galt als „zweites Rom". Ab 295 und während des gesamten 4. Jahrhunderts hielten die Kaiser sich häufig dort auf.

Landwirtschaft, Viehzucht und die von den Kelten ausgeübten Handwerke zogen die römischen Soldaten und Verwalter von Metz ebenso wie von Trier an. Notabeln und reiche Händler bauten komfortable Villae. Die Ruinen einer der prächtigsten von ihnen wurden 1975 in Schwaarz-uecht in der Nähe von Echternach entdeckt (rechte Seite), und im Jahre 1995 wurde in den Überresten einer Villa in Vichten ein herrliches Mosaik ausgegraben, das die neun Musen darstellt, die den Dichter Homer umgeben (folgende Doppelseite).

Andere aus gallo-römischen Villae stammende Mosaiken wurden in Diekirch gefunden. In Mamer, einem an der Straße von Trier nach Reims gelegenen Vicus wurden bei Ausgrabungen mit einem Hypocaust ausgestattete öffentliche Thermen und zahlreiche Skulpturen freigelegt. In Steinsel erhob sich mitten im Wald ein gallo-römischer Tempel, der von mehreren Gebäuden des 1. bis 4. Jahrhunderts umgeben ist. Von der großen Villa von Mersch am Zusammenfluss von Alzette und Eisch sind Hypocaust und ein Teil des enormen 75 Meter langen Beckens erhalten.

Bei den Ausgrabungen in den Ruinen der landwirtschaftlichen Villa von Koerich (vorhergehende Doppelseite) zeigte sich, dass es im 1. Jahrhundert eine große, von einer Befestigungsanlage umgebene Gruppe von Gebäuden gegeben hatte. Die beim Tëtelbierg in der Nähe von Rodange gefundenen Überreste der keltischen Oppidum (weiter oben) von fast drei Kilometern Umfang stammen aus dem 1. Jahrhundert vor Christus. Das Verteidigungsbauwerk wurde anschließend von den Römern besetzt. Zu all diesen Überresten kommen die Votivaltäre, zum Beispiel derjenige, der in der Kirche von Berdorf (Seite 28 bis 37) zu sehen ist, die Grabmonumente, die mit Reliefen verzierten Stelen, die Statuen der Gottheiten, die Gegenstände des täglichen Lebens und die Münzen mit dem Bildnis der verschiedenen Kaiser hinzu.

Unter dem Schutz der Pax Romana hielt das Christentum gleichzeitig mit dem Weinbau in das Land Einzug.

Im Jahre 395 wurde die Präfektur der Gallier von Trier nach Arles verlegt. Dies war das Ende des römischen Einflusses auf das Gebiet.

The Imprint of Rome

A NUMBER of circumstances made it easy for Roman civilization to be established in Luxembourg. Two great Roman roads linked Trier with Lyon and Rheims while another lead to Cologne. Trier, very close to the future Luxembourg was founded by the emperor Augustus in 15 BC and was considered "a second Rome". Roman emperors often stayed there from 295 through the IVth century.

Agriculture, cattle raising and the crafts pursued by the Celts attracted Roman soldiers and administrators from Metz as well as Trier. Prominent persons and wealthy merchants built comfortable villae. The ruins of one of the most sumptuous were discovered at Schwaarzuecht near Echternach in 1975 (below) and in 1995 a splendid mosaic representing the nine Muses surrounding Homer was discovered in the vestiges of a villa at Vichten (next double page).

Other mosaics were found in Gallo-Roman villas near Diekirch. At Mamer, a village on the road from Trier to Rheims, were public baths with a hypocaust and many sculptures were uncovered in the digs. At Steinsel a Gallo-Roman temple stood in the middle of the forest surrounded by several buildings from the Ist to the IVth centuries. All that remains of the great villa of Mersch, at the confluence of the Alzette and the Eisch, is the hypocaust and part of an enormous 75-meter long pool.

Excavations of the ruins of the farming villa of Koerich (preceding double page) have revealed that a great number of buildings surrounded by a rampart existed in the Ist century. Tëtelbierg, near Rodange, the remains of the Celtic oppidum (page left) nearly three kilometres in circumference date from the Ist century before Jesus Christ. The Romans later occupied this defensive work. To all these vestiges can be added votive altars such as the one found in the church of Berdorf (pages 28 to 37), funerary monuments, carved stelae, statues of the gods, everyday objects and coins stamped with the portraits of various emperors.

The pax romana made possible the introduction of Christianity at the same time as the introduction of viniculture.

In 395 the Prefecture of Gaul moved from Trier to Arles, thus ending the Roman hold on the territory.

De Stempel van Rome

A LLES droeg er toe bij om het pad te effenen voor de Romeinse beschaving in Luxemburg. Twee grote wegen verbonden Trier met Lyon en met Reims. Een derde liep naar Keulen. Vlakbij het toekomstige Luxemburg lag Trier, gesticht door keizer Augustus in 15 vóór Christus, en beschouwd als «het tweede Rome». Vanaf 295 en tijdens de hele vierde eeuw, verbleven de keizers er ook vaak.

Landbouw, veeteelt en de beroepen die de Kelten uitoefenden, trokken de Romeinse militairen en bestuurders aan uit Metz en uit Trier. Notabelen en rijke handelaars trokken er comfortabele villae op. De ruïnes van een wel zeer luxueuze villa werden in 1975 ontdekt in Schwaarzuecht bij Echternach (hier tegenover), en in 1995 werden de overblijfselen blootgelegd van een villa in Vichten, met prachtige mozaïeken waarop de negen muzen rond de dichter Homerus staan afgebeeld (volgende dubbele pagina).

Nog meer mozaïeken van Gallo-Romeinse villae werden ontdekt in Diekirch. In Mamer, een vicus op de heirbaan van Trier naar Reims, legden de opgravingen openbare badhuizen met een hypocaustum en talloze sculpturen bloot. In Steinsel, midden in het woud, prijkte een Gallo-Romeinse tempel, omgeven door gebouwen uit de eerste tot de vierde eeuw. Van de grote villa van Mersch aan de samenvloeiing van de Alzette en de Eisch resten nog het hypocaustum en een deel van het enorme bekken van 75 meter lang.

De opgravingen in de ruïnes van de villa van Koerich (voorgaande dubbele pagina) onthulden het bestaan, in de eerste eeuw, van een uitgestrekt geheel van bouwsels met een omwalling. Op de Tëtelbierg, bij Rodange, dateren de resten van het Keltisch oppidum (linkerbladzijde) met een omtrek van bijna drie kilometer, uit de eerste eeuw vóór Christus. Het bolwerk werd vervolgens ingenomen door de Romeinen. En dan zijn er nog de votiefaltaren, zoals bijvoorbeeld in de kerk van Berdorf (pagina 28 tot 37), de grafmonumenten, de gesculpteerde gedenkstenen, de beelden van godheden, de voorwerpen uit het dagelijks leven en de muntstukken met de beeltenis van de keizers.

Dankzij de pax romana kwam het christendom in het land, samen met de wijnteelt trouwens.

In 395 werd Arles de bestuurlijke hoofdstad van Gallië. Dat was het einde van de Romeinse greep op het grondgebied

DÈS le Vᵉ siècle avant Jésus-Christ, deux tribus celtiques se fixèrent de part et d'autre de la Moselle. Les Trévires occupaient la plus grande partie du futur Luxembourg, tandis que les Médiomatriques étaient établis plus au sud dans la région de Metz. Après la guerre des Gaules (58-50 avant Jésus-Christ) Trévires et Médiomatriques furent soumis à la domination romaine; la composition ethnique de la population ne se modifia guère mais elle fut profondément marquée par la civilisation romaine qui brillait à partir de Trèves et de Metz. En témoignent les vestiges de nombreuses *villae* et agglomérations, où ont été mis au jour mosaïques, autels votifs, sculptures et quantité d'objets usuels. La *pax romana* apporta une longue période de prospérité mais, après s'être emparé de Trèves en 460, Alamans et Francs Ripuaires s'y établirent et fusionnèrent avec les autochtones. Ils introduisirent leur langue, le *Moselfränkische*, dans la partie orientale du territoire où il sera à l'origine du parler luxembourgeois. Les Francs étant moins nombreux dans la partie occidentale du Luxembourg, le bas-latin s'y maintint. Il évoluera vers les dialectes romans.

Les Francs Ripuaires pratiquaient le culte d'Odin, ce qui menaçait de disparition le christianisme timidement implanté sous l'empire romain. Du moins jusqu'à la conversion et au baptême de Clovis, le Franc Salien qui conquit toute la Gaule entre 481 et 511. Sous les Mérovingiens, et davantage encore sous les Carolingiens, des missionnaires venus d'Aquitaine, d'Irlande et d'Angleterre entreprirent une ré-évangélisation complétée par l'activité des moines de nombreux monastères, notamment à Echternach où saint Willibrord fonda vers 711 une abbaye bénédictine qu'il organisa pour la formation religieuse des moines.

Le Luxembourg doit son nom à *Lucilinburhuc*, le «petit château». Il se dressait sur le rocher du Bock, qui dominait une boucle de l'Alzette proche du confluent avec la Pétrusse et de la chaussée romaine Reims-Trèves. En avril 963, Sigefroi, fils cadet du comte d'Ardenne, l'avait obtenu des moines de l'abbaye Saint-Maximin de Trèves en échange de son apanage de Feulen. On ne sait pas grand-chose de Sigefroi, sinon qu'il construisit un *castrum* et qu'il guerroya au service des empereurs germaniques. L'un de ses descendants prit le titre de comte de Luxembourg. Lorsque sa dynastie s'éteignit en 1136, le comté passa à Godefroid de Namur puis à son fils Henri l'Aveugle, un seigneur particulièrement ambitieux et turbulent. La fille de celui-ci, Ermesinde, fut la tige de la deuxième Maison de Luxembourg qui, entre 1308 et 1437, donna quatre empereurs au Saint-Empire de la nation germanique : Henri VII (r. 1308-1313), Charles IV (r. 1346-1378), Wenceslas (r. 1378-1400) et Sigismond (r. 1411-1437).

Entre-temps, le comté était devenu un duché. Région forestière demeurée pauvre malgré la gloire impériale des membres de sa maison régnante, le Luxembourg n'avait guère de ressources hormis les bois et le vin de ses vignobles le long de la Moselle. Cela explique que ses habitants restèrent soumis aux règles de la féodalité plus longtemps que les autres principautés qui l'entouraient. Les conflits sociaux étaient étrangers à la mentalité de la population; la première charte, celle d'Echternach, ne date que de 1236. La seconde fut octroyée à Luxembourg en 1243. Selon ces actes, les échevins et les bourgeois élisaient un justicier que le duc reconnaissait et installait officiellement. Il était chargé de veiller à la fois à la conservation de l'autorité ducale et au maintien des libertés des bourgeois.

En 1411, le duc de Luxembourg Wenceslas attribua le duché à son jeune frère Jean de Görlitz. La fille de celui-ci, Elisabeth, épousa Antoine de Bourgogne, duc de Brabant et de Limbourg. Le duché de Luxembourg englobait alors Thionville et Longwy aujourd'hui françaises, Chiny-sur-Semois, la terre de l'abbaye de Saint-Hubert, les seigneuries de La Roche et de Salm-Houffalize désormais en Belgique, ainsi que les plateaux s'étendant de la Sûre et de l'Our aux hauteurs de l'Eifel.

En 1441, moyennant la somme de 120 000 florins, la duchesse Elisabeth de Görlitz, veuve d'Antoine de Bourgogne, céda tous ses droits au duc de Bourgogne Philippe le Bon, son neveu par alliance, surnommé le «grand duc d'Occident». L'armée bourguignonne s'empara de la ville de Luxembourg sans que l'empereur germanique Frédéric IV ne formule aucune objection. Dès lors, le duché de Luxembourg partagea le destin des provinces que Philippe le Bon avait réussi à rassembler et dont l'empereur Charles Quint assura, au début du XVIᵉ siècle, la cohésion et l'autonomie sous le nom des Dix-Sept provinces des Pays-Bas, soit l'ensemble que formerait aujourd'hui le Luxembourg, la Belgique, les Pays-Bas et le nord de la France. Les députés luxembourgeois siégèrent aux États Généraux. Toutefois, la position excentrique du duché contribua à accentuer sa spécificité.

À l'écart des grands mouvements commerciaux concentrés sur les vallées de la Meuse et de l'Escaut, mais contrôlant l'accès aux Pays-Bas, Luxembourg ne tarda pas à devenir une puissante forteresse bastionnée. Le caractère militaire du duché lia le sort de ses habitants à celui de leurs souverains successifs auxquels ils témoignèrent un loyalisme indéfectible. À l'époque où le roi d'Espagne Philippe II, fils de Charles Quint, se trouvait aux prises avec la révolution politico-religieuse qui aboutit à la rupture des Dix-Sept provinces en Pays-Bas catholiques au sud — *grosso modo* la Belgique et le Luxembourg — et Provinces-Unies calvinistes au nord, les Luxembourgeois ne bronchèrent pas. Le prince Pierre-Ernest de Mansfeld, gouverneur du Luxembourg au nom de Philippe II, érigea dans la ville un remarquable monument de la Renaissance : l'actuel palais grand-ducal. Philippe II ordonna en outre la reconstruction de la moitié de la ville haute qui avait été ravagée par l'explosion d'une poudrière en 1504. Elle se fit avec rues rectilignes et larges. De l'urbanisme avant la lettre. À la fin de sa vie, Philippe II céda théoriquement les Pays-Bas espagnols, dont faisait partie le duché de Luxembourg, à sa fille Isabelle et à son époux l'archiduc Albert d'Autriche. Sous leur règne, la Contre-Réforme fut propulsée par les jésuites qui édifièrent, à côté de leur collège, une église qui deviendra la cathédrale Notre-Dame. À la même époque, les quelques cent entreprises sidérurgiques établies le long des cours d'eau atteignirent une production encore artisanale mais dépassant au total 200 tonnes de fontes.

Les archiducs Albert et Isabelle étant sans postérité, les Pays-Bas méridionaux retournèrent sous la souveraineté des Habsbourg d'Espagne. Les incessantes guerres de Louis XIV contre ceux-ci n'épargnèrent pas le duché. Le 7 novembre 1659, le traité des Pyrénées lui avait enlevé Thionville et Montmédy. Le 4 juin 1684, après un bombardement et un siège sanglant, le maréchal de Créqui s'empara de Luxembourg — au jour de la capitulation de la ville, l'armée française de 25 000 hommes se trouvait réduite à 17 000. Aussitôt après, Vauban entreprit de doter la place d'un vaste système de fortifications qui marquera à jamais le visage de la cité. Celle-ci bénéficia heureusement du déclin de l'hégémonie française : par le traité d'Utrecht, le 11 avril 1713, Louis XIV dut céder le duché de Luxembourg et toutes les provinces des Pays-Bas à l'empereur d'Autriche Charles VI. Les Habsbourg d'Autriche succédaient ainsi aux Habsbourg d'Espagne.

La Révolution française ayant repris à son compte les ambitions territoriales de Louis XIV, le 7 juin 1795, les troupes du général Jourdan s'emparèrent de la forteresse de Luxembourg après un siège de sept mois. Le Luxembourg devint, sous la République et l'Empire, le département des Forêts. La résistance à l'occupant s'y avéra intense. La «guerre des gourdins» — la *Köppelkrieg* — fut menée en coups de main acharnés mais elle était vouée à l'échec devant les Français très organisés. Quatre jours après l'abdication de Napoléon, Luxembourg ouvrit ses portes aux troupes alliées, le 15 avril 1815. Le pays portait encore la trace de ses souffrances. Les abbayes d'Orval et de Clairfontaine avaient été incendiées aux premiers jours de l'invasion française, l'abbaye d'Echternach avait été transformée en faïencerie.

Au Congrès de Vienne, les puissances victorieuses décidèrent de reconstituer un royaume des Pays-Bas, réunissant les provinces du nord et celles du sud sous le sceptre de Guillaume Iᵉʳ d'Orange-Nassau. Mais elles se virent contraintes par la Prusse de donner un statut spécial au Luxembourg : quelques principautés situées en terre de Nassau ayant été données au roi de Prusse, c'est par le principe de compensation que l'ancien duché de Luxembourg, élevé au rang de grand-duché, fut attribué à titre de propriété personnelle au roi des Pays-Bas. Toutefois, une armée prussienne de 4 000 hommes tiendrait garnison dans la forteresse. Loin de se soucier de l'appartenance théorique du grand-duché à la Confédération germanique, le roi-grand-duc Guillaume Iᵉʳ le considéra comme la dix-huitième province de son royaume. Quatre délégués luxembourgeois siégèrent d'ailleurs à la Chambre basse parmi les 55 députés des provinces méridionales. La population se montra plutôt satisfaite de son sort nouveau et demeura insensible aux griefs formulés contre la Maison d'Orange-Nassau. Les entraves à la liberté de la presse ne la préoccupaient pas; il n'y avait dans le Luxembourg qu'une seule gazette, rédigée en français et peu portée à la polémique. En revanche, la présence des 4 000 Prussiens dans la forteresse révulsait tout le monde sauf les petits commerçants.

Sans doute est-ce une des raisons pour lesquelles de nombreux patriotes luxembourgeois participèrent avec enthousiasme à la révolution belge de 1830. Le gouvernement provisoire du jeune État belge déclara sans hésiter que le Luxembourg faisait intégralement partie de la Belgique. Mais, en 1831, la Conférence de Londres s'opposa radicalement à cette réunion. Le traité des XXIV Articles scinda le Luxembourg en deux : la partie de parler germanique (2 586 km²) fut octroyée à Guillaume Iᵉʳ avec le titre de grand-duc, la partie majoritairement wallonne (4 439 km²) étant attribuée à la Belgique pour former la province belge du Luxembourg. Espérant obstinément un renversement de la situation, le roi de Hollande refusa d'adhérer au traité. Résultat : le Luxembourg tout entier demeura belge pendant plus de huit ans. Le 14 mars 1838, constatant enfin que la Belgique ne retournerait pas à la Maison d'Orange, le roi des Pays-Bas se résigna à accepter le traité de séparation.

La partition du Luxembourg prévue par le traité des XXIV Articles devint dès lors définitive en 1839. Elle fut ressentie comme frustrante par les grands-ducaux qui avaient la nostalgie d'un duché uni. Elle le fut aussi par les Belges qui avaient le souvenir tout proche d'une vie commune.

La tourmente révolutionnaire européenne de 1848 épargna la Belgique mais secoua quelque-peu la Hollande, dont le roi Guillaume II fut contraint de donner à ses peuples une constitution inspirée de celle de la Belgique. Son fils Guillaume III estima qu'il lui était difficile de gérer les affaires du grand-duché depuis La Haye. Il en confia le gouvernement — la «lieutenance» — à son frère Henri qui, par son équité et son écoute des sentiments de la population du Luxembourg, acquit promptement une réelle popularité.

L'empereur des Français Napoléon III comparait le Luxembourg à une seconde Savoie. Il rêvait de l'acheter à

Guillaume III qui était consentant et en avait fixé le prix à 5 millions de francs-or. Mais le grand-duché faisait toujours partie de la Confédération germanique et de l'Union douanière prussienne, le *Zollverein*. Par surcroît, le traité des XXIV Articles n'avait pas mis fin à la présence d'une garnison prussienne dans la forteresse. Une négociation s'imposait donc avec Bismarck, le chancelier du roi de Prusse. Celui-ci venait de vaincre l'Autriche à Sadowa et se sentait peu enclin aux concessions : les pourparlers traînèrent de novembre 1866 à avril 1867. Guillaume III avait lui aussi demandé son assentiment à la Prusse. Quand cette dernière se déroba en affirmant que le grand-duché était en quelque sorte englobé dans la neutralité belge, il déclara n'être plus vendeur. Napoléon III hésita à prendre une décision. La perspective d'une guerre franco-prussienne se dessinait. N'osant s'y lancer, l'empereur des Français proposa de rattacher le Luxembourg à la Belgique en échange des régions de Philippeville et de Mariembourg. Le gouvernement belge s'opposa évidemment à cette combinaison farfelue. Finalement Napoléon III accepta la réunion à Londres d'une conférence internationale qui décida la neutralisation du grand-duché sous la garantie des Puissances, le démantèlement des fortifications de la ville de Luxembourg et le départ de la garnison prussienne.

À la mort de Guillaume III en 1890, le pacte familial conclu en 1783 entre les différentes branches de la famille de Nassau et inclus dans les actes du Congrès de Vienne entra en application. Bien patrimonial des Nassau, le grand-duché de Luxembourg passa à Adolphe de Nassau-Weilbourg, dont le duché au nord du Main et à l'est du Rhin avait été annexé à la Prusse avec une compensation de plus de huit millions de tahlers. Ainsi prenait fin l'union personnelle du roi de Hollande et du grand-duc de Luxembourg.

Le fils d'Adolphe, Guillaume IV (r. 1904-1912) eut pour successeur l'aînée de ses filles, Marie-Adélaïde, qui fut acclamée comme la première souveraine née dans le pays.

Dès le règne de Guillaume III et la lieutenance de son frère le prince Henri, le Luxembourg avait initié sa période de prospérité économique grâce aux réseaux de chemin de fer vers Thionville et Arlon, puis vers Trèves. Il sortait de son isolement. Le coke importé de Liège permit d'abandonner bois et cours d'eau, les traditionnelles sources d'énergie des forges, pour transformer le minerais oolithique découvert par les frères Metz le long de la frontière avec la Lorraine française. La déphosphorisation du minerai, le procédé Thomas, se révéla décisive : la production de fonte dans les usines d'Esch-sur-Alzette atteignit un million de tonnes en 1900 et dépassa en 1913 deux millions et demi de tonnes, dont la moitié transformée en acier. La sidérurgie, dominante dans la vie économique, entraîna le développement ou permit le maintien d'industries moyennes dans les secteurs de la construction mécanique, la tannerie, la ganterie, la brasserie, la faïencerie, sans compter la viticulture. En même temps, le riche patrimoine culturel du pays et plus encore sa beauté naturelle très variée qui avaient séduit le poète Goethe et le peintre Turner attiraient de plus en plus de touristes.

En 1914, la neutralité du Luxembourg ne fut pas davantage respectée par les Allemands que celle de la Belgique. Le pays fut envahi sans coup férir. Toutefois, le gouvernement resta en place et les rouages de l'État continuèrent à fonctionner. Malgré ses traditionnels liens économiques avec l'Allemagne, la population ne cacha pas son hostilité aux occupants. Quelque 1 500 jeunes Luxembourgeois s'enrôlèrent dans l'armée française et près de 300 dans l'armée belge. À la libération du territoire, des groupes de meneurs excitèrent l'opinion publique défavorable à la grande-duchesse Marie-Adélaïde à qui l'on reprochait ses prétendus sentiments pro-allemands. L'agitation dégénéra en troubles graves, et Marie-Adélaïde abdiqua en faveur de sa sœur Charlotte. La question de la survie du grand-duché de Luxembourg se posa alors avec une certaine acuité. Des

Français organisèrent une intense et subtile propagande en faveur d'un rattachement à la république. De leur côté, quelques Belges regroupés en un 'comité de politique nationale' invoquaient l'Histoire bafouée selon eux en 1839. Les uns et les autres se méprenaient sur le réel sentiment national des Luxembourgeois, leur identité incontestable telle qu'exprimée par leur devise : *Mir wëlle bleiwe wat mir sin*, «Nous voulons rester ce que nous sommes».

Les nuages qui avaient obscurci les relations belgo-luxembourgeoises se dissipèrent par la promesse du roi des Belges Albert Ier d'apporter son appui illimité à Charlotte. Le 28 septembre 1919, un plébiscite organisé par le gouvernement luxembourgeois se traduisit par une écrasante majorité en faveur de la grande-duchesse Charlotte mais, résultat de la propagande française, par le même referendum les Luxembourgeois se prononcèrent majoritairement en faveur d'une union économique avec la France plutôt qu'avec la Belgique. Le maintien de garnisons françaises, que rien ne justifiait, mécontentait toutefois la population et, comme il fallait s'y attendre, le gouvernement britannique s'opposa à toute union franco-luxembourgeoise quelle qu'en soit la forme. En outre les puissants groupes industriels de Lorraine craignaient la concurrence des usines luxembourgeoises sur le marché intérieur français. L'Union économique belgo-luxembourgeoise (U.E.B.L.) fut signée le 1er mai 1921 et, à partir de 1935, le franc belge eut valeur dans le Luxembourg. Le commerce extérieur de l'U.E.B.L. prit un essor qui dépassa toutes les espérances. Les complémentarités lui permirent d'occuper en 1938 le rang de premier exportateur du monde de produits sidérurgiques et Luxembourg devint le siège du cartel international de l'acier.

Envahi en même temps que la Belgique et les Pays-Bas le 10 mai 1940, le Luxembourg subit durement les conséquences du fait que les nazis le considéraient comme une terre allemande. La grande-duchesse Charlotte et son gouvernement avaient pris le chemin de l'exil, le Gauleiter Gustave Simon avait les mains libres. À sa grande rage, lors du recensement-questionnaire du 10 octobre 1940 les Luxembourgeois rejetèrent massivement l'incorporation de leur pays au Reich. Réplique de l'occupant : à partir de 1942, douze mille jeunes gens furent contraints de se battre sous un uniforme et pour une cause qui n'étaient pas les leurs et 12 pour cent de la population furent déportés. La libération du territoire n'était pas totale lorsqu'en décembre 1944 le maréchal von Rundstedt déclencha son offensive dévastatrice, que repoussa la IIIe Armée américaine du général Patton. Le 13 février 1945 Vianden et Echternach étaient enfin libérées et, le 14 avril suivant, la grande-duchesse qui s'était réfugiée au Portugal puis aux États-Unis rentra triomphalement dans sa capitale.

Entre-temps, à Londres, le Luxembourgeois Joseph Bech, le Belge Paul-Henri Spaak et le Néerlandais E.N. van Kleffens avaient signé le 14 septembre 1944 les accords créant le Benelux. Dès lors, le Luxembourg participa activement avec ses deux partenaires à la longue marche vers l'unité européenne.

L'activité politique reprit promptement son cours traditionnel, malgré l'apparition d'un éphémère mouvement né de la Résistance, 'D'Union'. Les anciens partis se reconstituèrent sur des bases plus ou moins nouvelles : le parti chrétien-social qui fournit le plus grand nombre de chefs de gouvernement, parmi lesquels les figures internationales de Joseph Bech, Pierre Werner, Jacques Santer et Jean-Claude Juncker; le parti ouvrier socialiste qui connaîtra une scission au cours des années 1969-1971 sous le nom de parti social-démocrate; le parti libéral, rajeuni dans les années soixante par l'arrivée de personnalités comme Gaston Thorn (il présida ensuite la Commission de la C.E.E. à Bruxelles) et Colette Flesch; le parti communiste de plus en plus acculé à une position aussi vaine qu'intransigeante.

Dans l'histoire récente des relations sociales du Luxembourg, observent C. Calmes et D. Bossaert, il n'a été fait appel aux grèves que très exceptionnellement. Le recours à plusieurs organes de concertation et de consultation permet de les éviter. De toute évidence, ce climat de paix sociale est facilité par la prospérité économique du Luxembourg. Celle-ci est renforcée par l'importance de la place financière — 200 banques — due à une législation fiscale qui attire les capitaux. Le poids considérable du secteur bancaire a également contribué à compenser la crise des années 1970, qui menaçait la sidérurgie luxembourgeoise considérée comme la colonne vertébrale de l'économie, et favorisa des changements structurels, particulièrement en direction des services de radio-télévision et de télécommunication par satellites. De 1975 à 1992, une centaine de grandes entreprises nouvelles et performantes ont pu s'implanter au Luxembourg.

Les souverains luxembourgeois exercent leur action constitutionnelle en se tenant au-dessus de la mêlée politique, en dehors des luttes partisanes. «Ce n'est qu'avec la grande-duchesse Charlotte et grâce à elle, estime l'historien Gilbert Trausch, que la dynastie des Nassau-Weilbourg devient vraiment populaire. Son long règne montre l'influence que peut avoir un souverain qui règne mais ne gouverne pas.» En 1964, la grande-duchesse Charlotte abdiqua en faveur de son fils Jean qui avait épousé en 1953 la princesse Joséphine-Charlotte de Belgique, fille du roi Léopold III et de la reine Astrid.

L'aîné de leurs trois fils, le prince Henri, épousa le 14 février 1981 Maria Teresa Mestre. En 1998, le grand-duc Jean nomma Henri 'Lieutenant représentant' et, le 7 octobre 2000, il abdiqua en sa faveur. Le couple grand-ducal a quatre fils et une fille : les princes Guillaume, Félix, Louis, la princesse Alexandra et le prince Sébastien. Les 276 600 Luxembourgeois sont donc largement rassurés quant à la pérennité de la dynastie à laquelle ils ont toutes les raisons d'être profondément attachés.

IM 5. Jahrhundert vor Christus ließen sich zwei Keltenstämme zu beiden Seiten der Mosel nieder. Die Treverer besiedelten den größten Teil des künftigen Luxemburgs, während die Mediomatrici sich weiter im Süden in der Region Metz niederließen. Nach dem Gallischen Krieg (58-50 vor Christus) wurden Treverer und Mediomatrici von der römischen Herrschaft unterworfen. Die ethnische Zusammensetzung der Bevölkerung änderte sich kaum, wurde aber stark durch die römische Zivilisation geprägt, die sich von Trier und Metz aus verbreitete. Davon zeugen die Relikte zahlreicher *Villae* und Siedlungen, in denen Mosaiken, Votivaltäre, Skulpturen und zahlreiche Gebrauchsgegenstände ausgegraben wurden. Die *Pax romana* brachte eine lange Zeit des Wohlstands, aber nach der Eroberung von Trier im Jahre 460 ließen Alemannen und ripuarische Franken sich nieder und vermischten sich mit den Einheimischen. Im östlichen Teil des Gebiets führten sie das *Moselfränkische* ein, das die Grundlage der luxemburgischen Sprache sein wird. Im westlichen Teil waren die Franken weniger zahlreich, so dass sich dort das Spätlateinische hielt, aus dem später die romanischen Dialekte hervorgehen sollten.

Die ripuarischen Franken praktizierten den Odin-Kult, so dass das Christentum, das sich unter dem römischen Reich zaghaft ausgebreitet hatte, vom Aussterben bedroht war. Zumindest bis zur Konvertierung und Taufe des salischen Franken Chlodwig, der zwischen 481 und 511 ganz Gallien eroberte. Unter den Merowingern und mehr noch unter den Karolingern unternahmen aus Aquitanien, Irland und England stammende Missionare eine Reevangelisierung, die ergänzt wurde durch die Tätigkeit der Mönche aus zahlreichen Klöstern, insbesondere aus Echternach, wo der Heilige Willibrord um das Jahr 711 eine Benediktinerabtei gründete, die er auf die religiöse Ausbildung der Mönche ausrichtete.

Der Name Luxemburg geht auf *Lucilinburhuc* zurück, was "kleines Kastell" bedeutet. Es erhob sich auf dem Bockfelsen, der eine Kehre der Alzette in der Nähe des Zusammenflusses mit dem Bach Petrus und der römischen Straße, die von Reims nach Trier führte, beherrschte. Im April 963 hatte Sigfrid, der jüngste Sohn des Ardennergrafen, dieses Kastell im Tausch gegen seinen Besitz Feulen von den Mönchen der Abtei Sankt Maximin von Trier erhalten. Über Sigfrid ist nicht viel bekannt, außer, dass er ein *Castrum* errichtete und im Dienste der germanischen Kaiser Krieg führte. Einer seiner Nachkommen nahm den Titel des Grafen von Luxemburg an. Als seine Dynastie im Jahre 1136 ausstarb, ging die Grafschaft an Gottfried von Namur und anschließend an seinen Sohn Heinrich den Blinden, einen besonders ehrgeizigen und ausgelassenen Herrscher, über. Dessen Tochter Ermesinde war der Stamm des zweiten Hauses von Luxemburg, das dem Heiligen Reich deutscher Nation zwischen 1308 und 1437 vier Kaiser gab: Heinrich VII (Reg. 1308-1313), Karl IV (Reg. 1346-1378), Wenzel (Reg. 1378-1400) und Sigmund (Reg. 1411-1437).

Inzwischen war aus der Grafschaft ein Herzogtum geworden. Die Waldregion Luxemburg, die trotz des kaiserlichen Ruhmes der Mitglieder seines Herrscherhauses arm geblieben war, hatte mit Ausnahme der Wälder und des Weines seiner Weinberge entlang der Mosel kaum Ressourcen. Dies erklärt, dass seine Einwohner den Regeln der Feudalherrschaft länger unterlagen als die übrigen umliegenden Fürstentümer. Gesellschaftliche Konflikte waren der Mentalität der Bevölkerung fremd. Der erste Freibrief, der von Echternach, stammt erst aus dem Jahre 1236, der zweite wurde 1243 Luxemburg gewährt. Diesen Urkunden zufolge hatten Magistratsbeamten und Bürger einen Gerichtsherrn zu wählen, den der Herzog anerkannte und offiziell einsetzte. Aufgabe dieses Gerichtsherrn war es, sowohl auf die Wahrung der herzoglichen Macht als auch auf die der Freiheiten der Bürger zu achten.

1411 übertrug der Herzog von Luxemburg Wenzel das Herzogtum seinem jüngeren Bruder Johann von Görlitz. Dessen Tochter Elisabeth heiratete den Herzog von Brabant und Limburg, Anton von Burgund. Das Herzogtum Luxemburg umfasste damals die heute französischen Städte Thionville und Longwy, Chiny-sur-Semois, das Grundgebiet der Abtei von Saint-Hubert, die Lehnsherrschaften La Roche und Salm-Houffalize, heute Belgien zugehörig, sowie die Hochflächen, die sich von Sauer und Our bis zu den Höhen der Eifel erstreckten.

1441 übertrug die Herzogin Elisabeth von Görlitz, die Witwe von Anton von Burgund, für einen Betrag von 120.000 Gulden alle ihre Rechte an ihren angeheirateten Neffen, den Herzog von Burgund Philipp den Guten. Die burgundische Armee nahm die Stadt Luxemburg ein, ohne dass der germanische Kaiser Friedrich IV etwas dagegen unternahm. Von da an teilte das Herzogtum Luxemburg das Schicksal der Provinzen, die Philipp der Gute zusammenzubringen vermocht hatte und deren Zusammenhalt und Autonomie Kaiser Karl V Anfang des 16. Jahrhunderts unter dem Namen „Siebzehn Provinzen der Niederlande" gewährleistete. Es handelte sich dabei um die Einheit, die heute durch Luxemburg, Belgien, die Niederlande und Nordfrankreich gebildet wird. Die luxemburgischen Volksvertreter tagten in den Generalständen. Die abgelegene Position des Herzogtums trug jedoch zur Betonung seiner Besonderheit bei.

Luxemburg, das abseits der sich auf die Täler von Maas und Schelde konzentrierenden großen Handelsbewegungen lag, dafür aber den Zugang zu den Niederlanden kontrollierte, wurde bald zu einer starken Bollwerkfestung. Der militärische Charakter des Herzogtums verband das Schicksal seiner Einwohner mit dem ihrer aufeinander folgenden Herrscher, denen sie eine beständige Ergebenheit erwiesen. Als der König von Spanien, Philipp II, Sohn von Karl V, sich mit der politisch-religiösen Revolution auseinanderzusetzen hatte, die zum Zerfall der Siebzehn Provinzen in die katholischen Niederlande im Süden und in die kalvinistischen Vereinigten Provinzen im Norden führte, rührten die Luxemburger sich nicht. Ihr Gouverneur Prinz Peter-Ernst von Mansfeld errichtete in der Stadt ein denkwürdiges Bauwerk der Renaissance: den heutigen Großherzoglichen Palast. Philipp II ordnete zudem den Wiederaufbau der Hälfte der Oberstadt an, die im Jahre 1504 durch eine Pulverexplosion zerstört worden war. Der Wiederaufbau erfolgte in geradlinigen und breiten Straßen. Es war Städtebau, bevor es den Begriff überhaupt gab. Am Ende seines Lebens trat Philipp II die spanischen Niederlande, denen auch das Herzogtum Luxemburg angehörte, theoretisch an seine Tochter Isabella und deren Ehemann Erzherzog Albert von Österreich ab. Unter ihrer Herrschaft wurde die Gegenreform von den Jesuiten vorangetrieben, die neben ihrem Kollegium eine Kirche errichteten, die zur Kathedrale Unserer Lieben Frau werden sollte. Zu derselben Zeit erwirtschafteten die rund hundert entlang den Wasserläufen niedergelassenen Eisenhütten eine — zwar noch handwerkliche — Produktion, die aber bereits ein Gesamtvolumen von über 200 Tonnen Eisenguss erreichte.

Da die Erzherzöge Albert und Isabella keine Nachkommen hatten, kehrten die südlichen Niederlande wieder unter die Herrschaft der spanischen Habsburger zurück. Von den unablässigen Kriegen von Ludwig XIV gegen die Habsburger blieb auch das Herzogtum nicht verschont. Am 7. November 1659 hatte der Pyrenäen-Vertrag ihm Thionville und Montmédy genommen. Am 4. Juni 1684 bemächtigte sich Marschall Créqui nach einer Bombardierung und einer blutigen Belagerung Luxemburgs. Am Tage der Kapitulation der Stadt war die französische Armee von 25.000 Männern auf 17.000 dezimiert. Unmittelbar danach stattete Vauban die Stadt mit einem umfangreichen Befestigungssystem aus, das das Stadtbild seither prägt. Glücklicherweise kam der Stadt der Niedergang der französischen Vorherrschaft zugute: Mit dem Vertrag von Utrecht musste Ludwig XIV das Herzogtum Luxemburg und alle Provinzen der Niederlande am 11. April 1713 an den österreichischen Kaiser Karl VI abtreten. So folgten die österreichischen Habsburger auf die spanischen Habsburger.

Da die Französische Revolution die territorialen Ambitionen von Ludwig XIV übernommen hat, bemächtigten sich die Truppen von General Jourdan nach einer sieben Monate währenden Belagerung am 7. Juni 1795 der Festung Luxemburg. Unter der Republik und dem Kaiserreich wurde Luxemburg zum „Département des Forêts". Der Widerstand gegenüber der Besatzungsmacht erwies sich als stark. Der *Klöppelkrieg* wurde mit erbitterten Gefechten geführt, war aber zum Scheitern verurteilt, da die Franzosen ausgesprochen gut organisiert waren. Vier Tage nach der Abdankung Napoleons öffnete Luxemburg am 15. April 1815 den Truppen der Alliierten seine Tore. Das Land trug noch die Spur seiner Leiden: Die Abteien von Orval und Clairfontaine waren in den ersten Tagen der französischen Invasion angezündet worden, und die Abtei von Echternach war in eine Steingutfabrik verwandelt worden.

Auf dem Wiener Kongress beschlossen die Siegermächte, ein Königreich der Niederlande wiederherzustellen, dem die Provinzen des Nordens und des Südens unter dem Zepter von Wilhelm I von Oranien-Nassau angehören sollten. Aber sie wurden von Preußen dazu gezwungen, Luxemburg einen Sonderstatus zu geben: Da einige im Nassau-Gebiet liegende Fürstentümer dem König von Preußen zugesprochen worden waren, wurde das in den Rang eines Großherzogtums erhobene ehemalige Herzogtum Luxemburg als Ausgleich dem König der Niederlande als persönliches Eigentum zugewiesen. Eine 4.000 Mann starke preußische Armee sollte jedoch in der Festung in Garnison liegen. Weit davon entfernt, sich um die theoretische Zugehörigkeit des Großherzogtums zur germanischen Konföderation zu kümmern, betrachtete der König und Großherzog Wilhelm I es als achtzehnte Provinz seines Königreichs. Unter den 55 Volksvertretern der südlichen Provinzen tagten übrigens vier luxemburgische Vertreter im Unterhaus. Die Bevölkerung zeigte sich mit ihrem neuen Schicksal eher zufrieden und gegenüber den an das Haus von Oranien-Nassau gerichteten Beschwerden unempfindlich. Die Beschränkungen der Pressefreiheit kümmerten sie nicht. Es gab in Luxemburg nur eine einzige, auf Französisch erscheinende Zeitung, die nur wenig zu Streitbarkeit neigte. Die Anwesenheit der 4.000 Preußen in der Festung hingegen missfiel mit Ausnahme der kleinen Händler allen sehr.

Vermutlich ist dies einer der Gründe dafür, aus denen zahlreiche luxemburgische Patrioten mit Begeisterung an der belgischen Revolution von 1830 teilnahmen. Die provisorische Regierung des jungen belgischen Staats erklärte ohne zu Zögern, dass Luxemburg vollständig zu Belgien gehöre. Im Jahre 1831 widersetzte die Londoner Konferenz sich dieser Vereinigung jedoch vehement. Der 24-Artikel-Vertrag teilte Luxemburg in zwei Teile: Der die germanische Mundart sprechende Teil (2.586 km²) wurde Wilhelm I mit dem Titel eines Großherzogs zugewiesen, während der mehrheitlich wallonische Teil (4.439 km²) Belgien zugewiesen wurde, um die belgische Provinz Luxemburg zu bilden. Der König von Holland, der hartnäckig auf eine Umkehrung der Situation hoffte, weigerte sich, dem Vertrag zuzustimmen. Ergebnis: Ganz Luxemburg blieb über acht Jahre lang belgisch. Am 14. März 1838 erklärte sich der König der Niederlande bereit, den Teilungsvertrag anzuerkennen, da er

schließlich einsah, dass Belgien nicht zum Haus von Oranien zurückkehren würde.

Die im 24-Artikel-Vertrag vorgesehene Teilung von Luxemburg wurde im Jahre 1839 endgültig. Sie wurde von den Einwohnern des Großherzogtums, die sich nach einem vereinten Herzogtum sehnten, als frustrierend empfunden. Dies war auch bei den Belgiern der Fall, denen das gemeinsame Leben noch gut in Erinnerung war.

Die Wirren der europäischen Revolution von 1848 verschonten Belgien, erschütterten aber Holland, dessen König Wilhelm II gezwungen war, seinen Völkern eine Verfassung zu geben, die auf der Belgiens basierte. Sein Sohn Wilhelm III vertrat die Auffassung, dass es für ihn schwierig sei, die Geschäfte des Großherzogtums von Den Haag aus zu verwalten. Er übertrug die Regierung - die "Statthalterschaft" - seinem Bruder Heinrich, der durch seine Gerechtigkeit und seine Bereitschaft, die Anliegen der luxemburgischen Bevölkerung anzuhören, sofort echte Beliebtheit erwarb.

Der Kaiser der Franzosen Napoleon III verglich Luxemburg mit einem zweiten Savoyen. Er träumte davon, es Wilhelm III abzukaufen, der zustimmte und den Preis auf fünf Millionen Goldfranken festlegte. Aber das Großherzogtum war weiterhin Teil der germanischen Konföderation und des preußischen *Zollvereins*. Darüber hinaus hatte der 24-Artikel-Vertrag der Präsenz einer preußischen Garnison in der Festung kein Ende gesetzt. Daher war eine Verhandlung mit dem Kanzler des Königs von Preußen Bismarck erforderlich. Dieser hatte jedoch gerade Österreich in Sadowa besiegt und war kaum zu Zugeständnissen bereit: So zogen sich die Verhandlungen von November 1866 bis April 1867 hin. Auch Wilhelm III hatte Preußen um seine Zustimmung gebeten. Als Preußen auswich, indem es behauptete, das Großherzogtum sei in gewisser Weise in die belgische Neutralität integriert, erklärte er, nicht mehr verkaufen zu wollen. Napoleon III zögerte, eine Entscheidung zu treffen. Es zeichnete sich ein Krieg zwischen Frankreich und Preußen ab. Da er es nicht wagte, sich darauf einzulassen, schlug der Kaiser der Franzosen vor, Luxemburg im Tausch gegen die Regionen Philippeville und Mariembourg an Belgien anzugliedern. Die belgische Regierung widersetzte sich dieser eigenartigen Kombination natürlich. Schließlich akzeptierte Napoleon III die Einberufung einer internationalen Konferenz in London, die die Neutralisierung des Großherzogtums unter dem Schutz der Mächte, das Schleifen der Befestigungen der Stadt Luxemburg und den Abzug der preußischen Garnison beschloss.

Mit dem Tod Wilhelms III im Jahre 1890 wurde der 1783 zwischen den verschiedenen Zweigen der Familie von Nassau geschlossene Familienpakt, der in die Urkunden des Wiener Kongresses aufgenommen worden war, wirksam. Wenngleich es den Nassauern gehörte, ging das Großherzogtum Luxemburg auf Adolf von Nassau-Weilburg über, dessen Herzogtum nördlich des Mains und östlich des Rheins gegen eine Entschädigung von über acht Millionen Talern an Preußen angegliedert worden war. So endete die Personalunion des Königs von Hollands und des Großherzogs von Luxemburg.

Nachfolgerin des Sohnes von Adolf, Wilhelm IV (Reg. 1904-1912), war seine älteste Tochter Maria Adelheid, die als erste im Lande geborene Herrscherin eingesetzt wurde. Mit der Herrschaft von Wilhelm III und der Statthalterschaft seines Bruders Prinz Heinrich begann in Luxemburg dank des Eisenbahnnetzes nach Thionville und Arlon und später nach Trier die Zeit des wirtschaftlichen Aufschwungs. Das Land fand aus seiner Isolation heraus. Dank des aus Lüttich importierten Koks konnte man auf Holz und Wasserläufe, die traditionellen Energiequellen der Hüttenwerke zur Verarbeitung des von den Brüdern Metz entlang der Grenze zum französischen Lothringen gefundenen oolithischen Erzes verzichten. Als entscheidend erwies sich die Entphosphorung des Erzes, das Thomasverfahren: Die Erzeugung von Eisenguss in den Werken von Esch-sur-

Alzette erreichte im Jahre 1900 ein Volumen von einer Million Tonnen und überstieg 1913 zweieinhalb Millionen Tonnen, von denen die Hälfte zu Stahl verarbeitet wurde. Das Eisenhüttenwesen, ein dominierender Faktor des Wirtschaftslebens, führte zur Weiterentwicklung bzw. erlaubte die Beibehaltung mittelgroßer Betriebe in den Sektoren Maschinenbau, Lohgerberei, Handschuhindustrie, Braugewerbe und Steingutgewerbe sowie im Weinbau. Gleichzeitig zog das reiche Kulturerbe des Landes und mehr noch seine sehr vielfältige natürliche Schönheit, die den Dichter Goethe und den Maler Turner verzückt hatten, mehr und mehr Touristen an.

Im Jahre 1914 wurde die Neutralität Luxemburgs von den Deutschen ebenso wenig respektiert wie die Belgiens. Das Land wurde kampflos eingenommen. Die Regierung blieb jedoch im Amt, und die Räder des Staates funktionierten weiter. Trotz der traditionellen Wirtschaftsbeziehungen zu Deutschland verbarg die Bevölkerung nicht ihre Feindseligkeit gegenüber der Besatzungsmacht. Rund 1.500 junge Luxemburger traten der französischen und knapp 300 der belgischen Armee bei. Bei der Befreiung des Gebiets stachelten Gruppen von Aufrührern die negative Meinung der Öffentlichkeit über Großherzogin Maria Adelheid an, der man ihre angebliche deutschfreundliche Gesinnung vorwarf. Die Unruhe artete in schwere Ausschreitungen aus, und Maria Adelheid dankte zugunsten ihrer Schwester Charlotte ab. Nun stellte sich die Frage nach dem Überleben des Großherzogtums Luxemburg. Von den Franzosen wurde eine intensive und subtile Propaganda zugunsten einer Angliederung an die Republik durchgeführt. Einige zu einem ‚nationalpolitischen Ausschuss' zusammengeschlossene Belgier machten ihrerseits die ihrer Meinung nach im Jahre 1839 missachtete Geschichte geltend. Beide Seiten täuschten sich im Nationalgefühl der Luxemburger, in ihrer unbestreitbaren Identität, die in ihrer Devise *Mir wëlle bleiwe wat mir sin*, wir wollen bleiben, was wir sind, zum Ausdruck kommt.

Die Wolken, die die belgisch-luxemburgischen Beziehungen getrübt hatten, verzogen sich infolge des Versprechens des Königs der Belgier Albert I, Charlotte seine uneingeschränkte Unterstützung zu gewähren. Am 28. September 1919 ergab eine von der luxemburgischen Regierung durchgeführte Volksbefragung eine überwältigende Mehrheit zugunsten von Großherzogin Charlotte, aber aufgrund der französischen Propaganda sprachen sich die Luxemburger bei demselben Entscheid mehrheitlich für eine Wirtschaftsunion mit Frankreich und nicht mit Belgien aus. Die durch nichts gerechtfertigte Beibehaltung französischer Garnisonen stieß bei der Bevölkerung jedoch auf Kritik, und wie zu erwarten war, widersetzte sich die britische Regierung jeder wie auch immer gearteten französisch-luxemburgischen Union. Darüber hinaus fürchteten die mächtigen Industriekonzerne Lothringens die Konkurrenz der luxemburgischen Werke auf dem französischen Binnenmarkt. Die belgisch-luxemburgische Wirtschaftsunion (BLWU) wurde am 1. Mai 1921 besiegelt, und ab 1935 war der belgische Franc in Luxemburg als Währung im Umlauf. Der Außenhandel der BLWU nahm einen Aufschwung, der alle Erwartungen übertraf. Dank der Komplementaritäten wurde sie 1938 zum weltweit größten Exporteur von Erzeugnissen der Eisen- und Stahlindustrie, und Luxemburg wurde Sitz des internationalen Stahlkartells.

Luxemburg, in das die Deutschen am 10. Mai 1940 gleichzeitig mit Belgien und den Niederlanden einmarschierten, hatte schwer unter den Auswirkungen der Tatsache zu leiden, dass die Nazis es als deutschen Boden betrachteten. Großherzogin Charlotte und ihre Regierung waren ins Exil gegangen, so dass Gauleiter Gustav Simon freie Hand hatte. Zu seiner großen Empörung lehnten die Luxemburger beim Volkszählungsfragebogen vom 10. Oktober 1940 die Eingliederung ihres Landes ins Reich massiv ab. Reaktion der Besatzungsmacht: Ab 1942 wurden zwölftausend junge Menschen dazu gezwungen, in Uniform für eine Sache zu kämpfen, die nicht die ihre war, und 12% der Bevölkerung wurden deportiert. Die Befreiung des Gebiets war noch nicht abgeschlossen, als Marschall von Rundstedt im Dezember 1944 seine zerstörerische Offensive startete, die von der III. amerikanischen Armee von General Patton zurückgeschlagen wurde. Am 13. Februar 1945 waren Vianden und Echternach endlich befreit, und am folgenden 14. April kehrte die Großherzogin, die sich nach Portugal und dann in die Vereinigten Staaten geflüchtet hatte, im Triumph in ihre Hauptstadt zurück.

In der Zwischenzeit hatten der Luxemburger Joseph Bech, der Belgier Paul-Henri Spaak und der Niederländer E.N. van Kleffens am 14. September 1944 in London die Verträge zur Gründung von Benelux unterzeichnet. Von da an leistete Luxemburg mit seinen beiden Partnern einen aktiven Beitrag zum langen Weg zur europäischen Einheit.

Trotz des Aufkommens der aus der Résistance hervorgegangenen kurzlebigen Bewegung ‚D'Union' nahm die politische Tätigkeit bald wieder ihren gewohnten Lauf. Die alten Parteien bildeten sich auf mehr oder weniger neuen Grundlagen wieder neu: die christlich-soziale Partei, die die größte Zahl an Regierungschefs hervorbrachte, unter anderem die internationalen Persönlichkeiten Joseph Bech, Pierre Werner, Jacques Santer und Jean-Claude Juncker; die sozialistische Arbeiterpartei, die in den Jahren 1969-1971 unter dem Namen sozial-demokratische Partei eine Spaltung erleben wird; die liberale Partei, die in den sechziger Jahren durch Persönlichkeiten wie Gaston Thorn (der anschließend den Vorsitz der Kommission der EWG in Brüssel übernimmt) und Colette Flesch eine Verjüngung erfährt; die kommunistische Partei, die immer mehr zu einer ebenso vergeblichen wie unnachgiebigen Position gezwungen wird.

In der jüngsten Geschichte der sozialen Beziehungen Luxemburgs, so C. Calmes und D. Bossaert, kam es nur in Ausnahmefällen zu Streiks. In der Regel konnten sie durch mehrere Konzertierungs- und Konsultationsorgane vermieden werden. Dieses Klima des sozialen Friedens wird natürlich auch durch den wirtschaftlichen Wohlstand Luxemburgs begünstigt. Diese Prosperität wird durch die Bedeutung des luxemburgischen Finanzplatzes — 200 Banken — bedingt durch das Kapital anziehende Steuergesetzgebung gestärkt. Das beträchtliche Gewicht des Bankensektors trug auch zur Kompensierung der Krise der 70er Jahre bei, die die luxemburgische Eisen- und Stahlindustrie, die als Rückgrat der Wirtschaft gilt, bedrohte. Zudem begünstigte es den strukturellen Wandel, insbesondere zugunsten der Rundfunk-, Fernseh- und Satellitenkommunikationsdienste. Zwischen 1975 und 1992 haben sich rund hundert weitere leistungsfähige Unternehmen in Luxemburg niederlassen können.

Die luxemburgischen Herrscher üben ihr verfassungsmäßiges Amt aus, indem sie sich über politischen Streitigkeiten und Parteikämpfen halten. „Erst mit und dank Großherzogin Charlotte", so der Historiker Gilbert Trausch, „wird die Dynastie der Nassau-Weilburg wirklich beliebt. Ihre lange Herrschaft zeigt den Einfluss, den ein Herrscher haben kann, der herrscht, aber nicht regiert." Im Jahre 1964 dankte Großherzogin Charlotte zugunsten ihres Sohnes Jean ab, der 1953 Prinzessin Josephine-Charlotte von Belgien, die Tochter von König Leopold III und Königin Astrid geheiratet hatte.

Der älteste ihrer drei Söhne, Prinz Henri, heiratete am 14. Februar 1981 Maria Teresa Mestre. 1998 ernannte Großherzog Jean Henri zum Statthalter, und am 7. Oktober 2000 dankte er zu seinen Gunsten ab. Das großherzogliche Paar hat vier Söhne und eine Tochter: die Prinzen Guillaume, Felix und Louis, die Prinzessin Alexandra und den Prinzen Sebastian. Die 276.600 Luxemburger können in Bezug auf den Fortbestand ihres Herrschergeschlechts, dem sie sich ganz zu Recht sehr verbunden fühlen, also vollkommen beruhigt sein.

AROUND the fifth century before the Christian era, two Celtic tribes settled on either side of the Moselle. The Treveri occupied the greater part of the future Luxembourg while the Mediomatrici were settled more to the south in the region of Metz. After the Gallic War (58-50 BC) both the Treveri and the Mediomatrici fell under Roman rule. The ethnic composition of the population barely changed but it was profoundly influenced by the Roman civilization established in Trier and Metz. The remains of a number of *villae* and settlements where mosaics, votive altars, sculptures and numerous everyday objects have been uncovered confirm this. The *pax romana* afforded a long period of prosperity but after the Allemans and Ripuarian Franks seized Trier in 460 AD they settled the area and intermarried with the natives. They introduced the *moselfränkische* in the eastern part of the territory which would be the origin of the Luxembourg language, the Letzebuergish. As the Franks were less numerous in the western part, Vulgar Latin continued to be spoken, developing into Romanic dialects.

The Ripuarian Franks worshipped Odin, thus menacing Christianity, feebly implanted under the Roman Empire until the conversion and baptism of Clovis, the Salic Frank, who conquered all of Gaul between 481and 511. Under the Merovingians, and particularly under the Carolingians, missionaries from Aquitaine, Ireland and England undertook a new evangelisation aided by the activity of the monks of the many monasteries. One of the most notable was the Benedictine abbey of Echternach, founded around 711 by Saint Willibrord as a seminary.

Luxembourg owes its name to *Lucilinburhuc*, the "little fortress", standing on the rocky eminence of the Bock, dominating a bend of the Alzette river, close to its confluence with the Petrusse and the Roman road between Reims and Trier. In April, 963, Sigefroid, the youngest son of the Count of Ardenne received it from the monks of the abbey of Saint Maximin of Trier in exchange for his appanage of Feulen. Not much is known of him other than he built a *castrum* and that he fought for the Holy Roman Emperors. One of his descendants took the title of Count of Luxembourg. When his dynasty expired in 1136 the county passed to Godefroid of Namur and then to his son, Henry the Blind, a particularly ambitious and unruly lord. His daughter, Ermensinde, founded the line of the second House of Luxembourg, which, between 1308 and 1437 provided four Emperors to the Germanic Holy Roman Empire: Henry VII (reigned 1308-13), Charles IV (r. 1346-1378), Wenceslas (r.1378-1400) and Sigismond (r.1411-1437).

In the meantime the County had become a Duchy. The heavily forested region remained poor, despite the Imperial glory of its ruling house. Luxembourg had hardly any resources other than wood and the wine of its vineyards along the Moselle. For this reason its inhabitants remained under the yoke of feudalism longer than the other principalities around it. Social conflict was foreign to the nature of the population. The first Charter, that of Echternach, dates only from 1236; the second was granted to Luxembourg in 1243. By these acts, aldermen and burghers elected a justiciar that the Duke accepted and installed officially in his functions. He was responsible for both conserving the ducal power and maintaining the freedom granted the burghers.

In 1411, the Duke of Luxembourg Wenceslas gave the Duchy to his young brother, John of Görlitz. His daughter Elizabeth married Anthony of Burgundy, Duke of Brabant and of Limbourg. The Duchy of Luxembourg at that time possessed Thionville and Longwy now French, Chiny-sur-Semois, the lands of the Abbey of Saint Hubert, the seignories of La Roche and of Salm-Houffalize now in Belgium as well as the plateaus stretching from the Sûre and the Eure to the heights of the Eifel.

In 1441 Duchess Elizabeth of Görlitz, widow of Anthony of Burgundy ceded all her rights to Philip the Good, Duke of Burgundy, her nephew by marriage, known as "the Grand Duke of the West", for 120,000 florins. Frederick IV, the Holy Roman Emperor did not object when the Burgundian army took over the city of Luxembourg. From then on the Duchy of Luxembourg shared the destiny of the provinces that Philip the Good had managed to unite and which under Emperor Charles the Fifth at the beginning of the 16th century became a cohesive and autonomous nation under the name of the Seventeen United provinces of the Low Countries, an ensemble which, if it existed today would be made up of Luxembourg, Belgium, the Netherlands and the north of France. Deputies from Luxembourg sat in the States General. Nevertheless, the outlying position of the Duchy preserved its distinctive nature.

Luxembourg, though remote from the important commercial regions of the valleys of the Meuse and the Scheldt, controlled the access to the Low Countries and quickly became a powerful, bastioned fortress. The military character of the Duchy tied the destiny of its inhabitants to that of their successive sovereigns to whom they were staunchly loyal. During the epoch of the Spanish king, Philip II, son of Charles the Fifth, who found himself at loggerheads with the politico-religious revolution which led to the scission of the Seventeen Provinces into the Catholic Low Countries to the south and the Calvinist United Provinces to the north, the Luxembourgers never wavered. Their Governor, Count Peter Ernest Mansfeld, erected a remarkable Renaissance building in the city, now the present Grand-Ducal palace. Philip II also commanded the reconstruction of the half of the upper town that had been destroyed by the explosion of a powder magazine in 1504. Rebuilt with wide, straight streets it is an early example of urban planning. At the end of his life Philip II ceded, in theory, the Spanish Netherlands of which the Duchy of Luxembourg was part to his daughter Isabelle and her husband, Archduke Albert of Austria. At this time some one hundred forges along the rivers produced, by artisanal methods, more than 200 tons of cast iron.

The Archdukes Albert and Isabelle were without issue and the southern Low Countries returned to rule by the Habsburgs of Spain. The continual wars of Louis XIV with Spain did not spare the Duchy. Thionville and Montmédy were taken from it by the Treaty of the Pyrenées on November 7, 1659. On June 4, 1684, after a bombardment and a bloody siege that reduced the French army from 25,000 men to 17,000, Maréchal de Crequi took the city. Shortly thereafter, Vauban began construction of a vast system of fortifications that would change forever the aspect of the city. Luxembourg benefited from the decline of French hegemony, however, as by the Treaty of Utrecht Louis XIV had to cede the Duchy and all the provinces of the Low Countries to Charles VI, the Emperor of Austria. Thus the Habsburgs of Austria succeeded the Habsburgs of Spain.

The French Revolution harboured the same territorial ambitions as Louis XIV and on June 7, 1795 the troops of General Jourdan took the fortress of Luxembourg after a seven month siege. Luxembourg became, under both the Republic and the Empire, the Department of Forests. There was intense resistance to the occupiers. The "War of the Sticks" — the Köppelkrieg — was fought bravely but was destined to fail before the well-organized French. Four days after Napoleon abdicated, Luxembourg opened its gates to the allied armies on April 15, 1815. The country still carried the scars of its occupation. The abbeys of Orval and of Clairfontaine had been burnt early in the French invasion and the abbey of Echternach had been turned into a pottery works.

At the Congress of Vienna the victorious powers decided to reconstitute a Kingdom of the Netherlands, reuniting the Northern and Southern provinces under the sceptre of William I of Orange-Nassau. However, they were forced by Prussia to give a special status to the former Duchy of Luxembourg. Since several principalities situated in the lands of Nassau had been given to the King of Prussia, the King of the Netherlands, by principle of compensation, was awarded Luxembourg, now elevated to a Grand Duchy, as his personal property. Nonetheless, a Prussian army garrison of 4000 men held the fortress. Far from worrying about the theoretical position of the Grand Duchy in the German Confederation, the King-Grand Duke William I considered it as the eighteenth province of his realm. Four Luxembourg delegates sat in the Lower Chamber along with 55 deputies from the southern provinces. The populace seemed to be rather content with its new condition and remained unmoved by the complaints raised against the House of Orange-Nassau. The control of the press didn't bother it, as there was only one newspaper in all of Luxembourg, written in French and not given to controversy. On the other hand, the 4000 Prussians in the fortress angered everyone, except the small businessmen.

This is probably one of the reasons that a great number of Luxembourg patriots participated enthusiastically in the Belgian Revolution of 1830. The Provisional Government of the young Belgian State declared immediately that Luxembourg was an integral part of Belgium. However, the London Conference of 1831 was totally opposed to this union. The Treaty of the XXIV Articles divided Luxembourg in two: the German-speaking region (2,586 km square) was given to William I with the title of Grand Duke. And the predominately Walloon region (4,439 km square) was given to Belgium to form the Belgian province of Luxembourg. Thus all of Luxembourg remained Belgian for eight years. Finally realizing that Belgium would not return to the House of Orange, the King of the Netherlands accepted the treaty of separation on March 14, 1838.

Thus the partition of Luxembourg laid out in the Treaty of XXIV Articles became definitive in 1839. This frustrated the people of the Grand Duchy who yearned for the old united Duchy. The Belgians who had recent memories of a common state also resented it.

The revolutionary throes of Europe in 1848 spared Belgium but had repercussions in Holland where King William II was forced to give his subjects a constitution similar to that of Belgium. His son, William III found it too difficult to administer the affairs of the Grand Duchy from The Hague and delegated his brother Henry as his Lieutenant to govern the territory. Henry, by his evenhandedness and willingness to listen to the people of Luxembourg quickly gained a real popularity.

The French Emperor Napoleon III esteemed that Luxembourg was a second Savoy and wanted to buy it from William III who was agreeable and fixed a price of 5 million gold francs. However, the Grand Duchy was still a member of the German Confederation and of the Prussian Customs Union, the *Zollverein*; furthermore, the Treaty of the XXIV Articles had not put an end to the Prussian garrison in the fortress. It was therefore necessary to negotiate with Bismarck, the Chancellor of the King of Prussia who had just defeated the Austrians at Sadowa and was not in a mood to make any concessions. Discussions dragged on from November 1866 to April 1867. William III had also asked for the consent of Prussia which evaded the question by stating that the Grand Duchy was more or less in the pact on Belgian neutrality. William decided not to sell, therefore. Napoleon III could not make up his mind as it might

lead to a Franco-Prussian war. Not daring to fight, the French Emperor proposed returning Luxembourg to Belgium in exchange for the regions of Philippeville and Mariembourg. The Belgian government strongly opposed this rather ridiculous proposition. Napoleon III finally accepted the deliberations of an international conference held in London that decided on a neutral status for the Grand Duchy, guaranteed by the Great Powers, the dismantlement of the fortifications of the city of Luxembourg and the withdrawal of the Prussian garrison.

When William III died in 1890 the family pact agreed upon by the different branches of the House of Nassau in 1783, and included in the acts of the Congress of Vienna, entered into force. The Grand Duchy of Luxembourg, the personal property of the House of Nassau, became the property of Adolph of Nassau-Weilbourg whose Duchy to the north of the Main and east of the Rhine had been annexed by Prussia with a compensation of 8 million thalers. Thus the union in one person of the King of Holland and of the Grand Duke of Luxembourg was terminated.

William III, the son of Adolph, ruled from 1904 to 1912 and was succeeded by his eldest daughter, Maria Adelheid, who was celebrated as being the first sovereign born in the country.

During the reign of William III and the lieutenancy of his brother, Prince Henry, Luxembourg, no longer isolated, entered into a period of economic prosperity, thanks to the network of railroads connecting it to Thionville and Arlon and later to Trier. Coke imported from Liège led to the abandoning of the traditional method of wood and water power as energy in the forges to transform the oolitic ore found along the border with French Lorraine by the Metz brothers. The elimination of phosphorus from the ore, by the Thomas, or basic open-hearth, process was paramount. The iron production of the factories of Esch-sur-Alzette reached a million tons in 1900 and more than two and a half million tons in 1913, half of it steel. The iron and steel industry dominated the economy and led to the establishment or the flourishing of medium-sized industries in the sectors of mechanical construction, tanning, glove making, brewing and pottery, not to mention viticulture. At the same time the rich cultural heritage of the country and particularly its varied, natural beauty that had already enchanted the poet Goethe and the artist, Turner, attracted more and more tourists.

In 1914 the Germans did not respect the neutrality of Luxembourg any more than that of Belgium. The country was invaded without any opposition. Nevertheless, the government remained in place and the wheels of State continued to turn. Despite the traditional economic ties with Germany the population did not hide its hostility to the occupiers. Some 1500 young Luxembourgers enlisted in the French army and around 300 in the Belgian army. When the territory was liberated some groups of agitators roused public opinion against the Grand Duchess Maria Adelheid whom they accused of pro-German sentiments. The agitation degenerated into a dangerous situation and Maria Adelheid abdicated in favour of her sister Charlotte. The survival of the Grand Duchy was in great danger. The French organized an intense, if subtle, propaganda campaign in favour of joining the Republic. On the Belgian side, a few Belgians formed a 'national policy committee' based on, according to them, the 'historical error' of 1839. Both sides misunderstood the true patriotic feelings of the people of Luxembourg whose national identity is well defined in their motto: *Mir wëlle bleiwe wat mir sin*, meaning, "We want to remain what we are".

The clouds hanging over the relations between Belgium and Luxembourg lifted when Albert I, King of the Belgians, gave his unlimited support to Charlotte. On September 28, 1919 a plebiscite organized by the Luxembourg government produced a crushing majority in favour of Grand Duchess Charlotte but also, resulting from the intense French propaganda, in the same referendum the citizens voted for an economic union with France rather than with Belgium. However, the presence of without any justification of a French garrison irritated the populace and, as was to be expected, the British government was opposed to a union of any sort between France and Luxembourg. Furthermore, powerful industrial groups in Lorraine feared the competition of the factories of Luxembourg in the domestic market. The economic union of Belgium and Luxembourg, the U.E.B.L., was signed on May 1, 1921 and in 1935 the Belgian franc was accepted at par in Luxembourg. The external commerce of the U.E.B.L. soared beyond all expectations. The complementarity of the two economies led to them being the largest exporters in the world of iron and steel in 1938 and Luxembourg became the seat of an international steel cartel.

Luxembourg, which was invaded on May 10, 1940 at the same time as Belgium and Holland, paid heavily for the fact that the Nazis considered it part of Germany's territory. Grand Duchess Charlotte and her government fled into exile and the Gauleiter, Gustave Simon had a free hand. Much to his fury, during the census-questionnaire of October 10, 1940, the people of Luxembourg rejected en masse being incorporated into the Reich. The occupiers replied by drafting twelve thousand youths into the German army in 1942 to fight for a cause that was not theirs and 12% of the population was deported. The territory had not been completely liberated when in December 1944 Marshal von Rundstedt began his devastating offensive, pushing back the American Third Army under General Patton. On February 13, 1945 Vianden and Echternach were finally liberated and on April 14 the Grand Duchess who had taken refuge in Portugal and later in the United States entered triumphantly into her capital.

In the meantime, Joseph Bech of Luxembourg, Paul-Henri Spaak of Belgium and E.N. van Kleffens of the Netherlands had signed the agreements forming the Benelux on September 14, 1944 in London. From that time on Luxembourg would be an active participant with its two partners on the long march towards European union.

Political activity immediately began in the traditional manner despite the appearance of an ephemeral movement, born of the Resistance, called 'D'Union'. The old parties were reconstituted on more or less new bases such as the Christian Socialist party that has provided the greatest number of heads of government among whom are the internationally known Joseph Bech, Pierre Werner, Jacques Santer and Jean-Claude Juncker; the Socialist Worker's party which underwent a split during the years 1969-71, taking the name of the Social Democratic party; the Liberal party, rejuvenated in the '60s by the arrival of people such as Gaston Thorn who would later preside over the Commission of the EEC in Brussels, and Colette Flesch. The Communist party was driven back into a position as futile as it was intransigent.

As is noted by C. Calmes and D. Bossaert in recent history strikes have occurred only rarely, as there are several organs for dialogue and consultation available. The peaceful social climate of Luxembourg is no doubt due to its economic prosperity. This is helped by the important financial sector - some 200 banks - benefiting from fiscal legislation that is attractive to capital. The considerable weight of the banking sector has also helped to compensate for the crisis of the '70s that threatened the iron and steel industry of Luxembourg, considered the backbone of the economy, and to effect structural change, particularly in the domains of radio and television and satellite telecommunications. From 1975 to 1992 some one hundred large, dynamic new firms have been established in Luxembourg.

The sovereigns of Luxembourg execute their constitutional roles by standing apart from the political sector, above partisan politics. "It is only with Grand Duchess Charlotte, and thanks to her," said the historian Gilbert Trausch, "that the dynasty of Nassau-Weilbourg became truly popular. Her long reign demonstrates the influence that a sovereign who reigns, but does not rule, can have." In 1964 Grand Duchess Charlotte abdicated in favour of her son Jean who had married Princess Josephine-Charlotte of Belgium, daughter of King Leopold III and Queen Astrid in 1953.

The eldest of their three sons, Prince Henry, married Maria Theresa Mestre on February 14, 1981. In 1998 The Grand Duke Jean named Henry as his "representative Lieutenant" and abdicated in his favour on October 7, 2000. The Grand Ducal couple has four sons and a daughter: the Princes William, Felix, Louis, Princess Alexandra, and Prince Sebastian. The 276,000 citizens of Luxembourg are thus assured of the longevity of the dynasty to which they are profoundly attached.

IN de vijfde eeuw vóór Christus vestigen zich twee Keltische stammen aan weerskanten van de Moezel. De Treveri bezetten het grootste deel van het toekomstige Luxemburg, terwijl de Mediomatricers neerstreken rond Metz, meer in het zuiden. Na de Gallische oorlog (58-50 vóór Christus) werden de Treveri en de Mediomatricers onderworpen aan de Romeinse heerschappij. Aan de etnische samenstelling van de bevolking veranderde weinig, maar ze werd wel sterk beïnvloed door de Romeinse beschaving, die in en rond Trier en Metz bloeide. Daarvan getuigen de overblijfselen van talrijke *villae* en agglomeraties waar heel wat mozaïekwerk, votiefaltaren, sculpturen en talloze gebruiksvoorwerpen werden gevonden. De *pax romana* bracht een lange periode van welvaart. Maar in 460 namen de Alamannen en de Ripuariërs Trier in. Ze bleven ter plaatse en vermengden zich met de vroegere bewoners. Zij brachten hun Frankische taal mee, het *Moselfränkisch*, dat ze oplegden in het oostelijk deel van het grondgebied, waar het aan de basis zal liggen van de Luxemburgse taal. De Franken waren minder talrijk in het westelijk gedeelte, waar dus het Laat-Latijn behouden bleef. Dit evolueerde dan naar de Romaanse dialecten.

De Ripuariërs vereerden de god Odin. Dat betekende een bedreiging voor het voorzichtig opkomende christendom onder de Romeinse overheersing. Maar de Salische Frank Clovis, die heel Gallië veroverde tussen 481 et 511, deed het tij keren toen hij zich bekeerde en liet dopen. Onder de Merovingers, en meer nog de Karolingers, begonnen missionarissen uit de Aquitaine, Ierland en Engeland aan een grootscheepse kerstening. Zij kregen steun van de monniken van talloze kloosters, meer bepaald in Echternach waar de heilige Willibrordus, omstreeks 711, een benedictijnerabdij stichtte met het oog op de religieuze vorming van de monniken.

Luxemburg dankt zijn naam aan het woord *Lucilinburhuc*, of «klein kasteel». Dit prijkte op de rots de Bock, die boven een lus van de Alzette uittorende, vlakbij de samenvloeiing met de Petrusse en de heirbaan die van Reims naar Trier liep. In april 963 kwam het in het bezit van Sigfrid, de jongste zoon van de graaf der Ardennen, die het had verworven van de monniken van de abdij Sankt Maximinus van Trier, in ruil voor zijn erfgoed Feulen. Er is weinig bekend over deze figuur, behalve dan dat hij een *castrum* bouwde en ten strijde trok in dienst van de Germaanse keizers. Eén van zijn afstammelingen nam de titel van graaf van Luxemburg aan. Toen zijn dynastie uitdoofde in 1136, ging het graafschap over naar Godfried van Namen en vervolgens naar diens zoon Hendrik de Blinde, een bijzonder ambitieus en woelig heerschap. Diens dochter, Ermesinde, was de tak van het Tweede Huis Luxemburg dat, tussen 1308 en 1437, vier Roomse Koningen leverde: Hendrik VII (r. 1308-1313), Karel IV (r. 1346-1378), Wenceslaus (r. 1378-1400) en Sigismund (r. 1411-1437).

Ondertussen was het graafschap een hertogdom geworden. Het sterk beboste Luxemburg was een arme streek gebleven, ondanks de keizerlijke roem van de leden van zijn regerend huis, en had maar weinig hulpbronnen buiten het woud en de wijn van zijn wijngaarden langs de Moezel. Dit verklaart waarom de bewoners langer dan de andere vorstendommen in de omgeving onderworpen bleven aan de feodale regels. Sociale conflicten pasten echter niet in de denkwereld van de bevolking. De eerste keure, van Echternach, komt er pas in 1236; de tweede werd verleend aan Luxemburg, in 1243. Deze akten bepaalden dat de wet-

houders en burgers een rechtshandhaver mochten kiezen, die de hertog dan erkende en officieel vestigde. Deze magistraat moest tegelijk waken over de vrijwaring van het hertogelijk gezag en van de vrijheden van de poorters.

In 1411 schonk de hertog van Luxemburg Wenceslaus het hertogdom aan zijn jonge broer Johan van Görlitz. Diens dochter, Elizabeth, huwde Antoon van Bourgondië, hertog van Brabant en Limburg. Het hertogdom Luxemburg omvatte toen Thionville en Longwy die nu Frans zijn, Chiny-sur-Semois, het grondgebied van de abdij van Saint-Hubert, de heerlijkheden van La Roche en van Salm-Houffalize die nu tot België behoren, en ook de plateaus die zich uitstrekken van de Sûre en de Our tot de hoogten van de Eifel.

In 1441 stond hertogin Elisabeth van Görlitz, weduwe van Antoon van Bourgondië, voor de som van 120 000 florijnen, al haar rechten af aan de hertog van Bourgondië, Filips de Goede, haar aangetrouwde neef die de bijnaam «Grote Hertog van het Westen» kreeg. Het Bourgondisch leger nam de stad Luxemburg in, zonder enig verzet van de Duitse keizer Frederik IV. Vanaf dat moment deelde het hertogdom het lot van de provincies die Filips de Goede samenvoegde en waarin keizer Karel, in het begin van de zestiende eeuw, samenhang bracht. Dit autonome blok kreeg de naam Zeventien Provinciën der Nederlanden en bestond uit het huidige Luxemburg, België, Nederland en het noorden van Frankrijk. De Luxemburgse afgevaardigden zetelden in de Staten-Generaal; maar omdat het hertogdom aan de zijlijn lag, bleef het zijn aparte eigenheid behouden.

Het had dan wel niet echt deel aan de handelsbewegingen die toegespitst waren op de valleien van de Moezel en van de Schelde, maar beheerste wel de toegang tot de Nederlanden en dus werd Luxemburg al snel een machtig bolwerk. Door het militaire karakter van het hertogdom raakten de inwoners telkens weer betrokken bij de lotgevallen van hun opeenvolgende vorsten, die ze onwankelbaar trouw bleven. Toen de Spaanse koning Filips II, zoon van Karel V, verwikkeld raakte in de politiek-religieuze revolutie die leidde tot de opdeling van de Zeventien Provinciën in de katholieke Nederlanden in het zuiden en de calvinistische Verenigde Provinciën in het noorden, gaven de Luxemburgers geen kik. Hun gouverneur, prins Peter Ernest van Mansfeld, liet in de stad een opmerkelijk renaissance-monument optrekken: het huidig groothertogelijk paleis. Filips II gaf daarbij ook het bevel om de helft van de bovenstad weer op te bouwen, na de verwoesting die de ontploffing van een munitieopslagplaats in 1504 aanrichtte. De nieuwe straten waren recht en breed, een staaltje stedenbouw avant la lettre. Op het einde van zijn leven stond Filips II theoretisch de Spaanse Nederlanden, waar het hertogdom Luxemburg toe behoorde, af aan zijn dochter Isabella en haar echtgenoot aartshertog Albrecht van Oostenrijk. Onder hun bewind zette de Contrareformatie fors op, door de Jezuïeten die naast hun college een kerk bouwden die later de Onze-Lieve-Vrouwkathedraal zou worden. In die zelfde tijd haalden de enkele honderden ijzer- en staalbedrijven langs de waterlopen een productie die weliswaar nog ambachtelijk was, maar toch in de buurt van 200 ton gietijzer kwam.

De aartshertogen Albrecht en Isabella bleven kinderloos en dus gingen de zuidelijke Nederlanden weer naar de Spaanse Habsburgers. De onophoudelijke oorlogen die Lodewijk XIV tegen hen voerde, spaarden het hertogdom niet. Op 7 november 1659 was hij door het verdrag van de Pyreneeën al Thionville en Montmédy kwijtgeraakt. Op 4 juni 1684 overmeesterde maarschalk de Créqui Luxemburg, na een bombardement en een bloedige belegering. Van de 25 000 manschappen die het Franse leger telde, restten er op de dag van de overgave nog slechts 17 000. Meteen daarna ging Vauban van start met de aanleg van een uitgebreid systeem van versterkingen die het gelaat van de stad eens voor al zouden bepalen. Gelukkig hield de Franse overheersing niet lang stand: met het verdrag van Utrecht, op 11 april

1713, moest Lodewijk XIV het hertogdom Luxemburg en alle provinciën van de Nederlanden overlaten aan de keizer van Oostenrijk, Karel VI. Zo volgden de Oostenrijkse Habsburgers de Spaanse Habsburgers op.

Ondertussen nam de Franse Revolutie de territoriale ambities van Lodewijk XIV over en op 7 juni 1795 veroverden de troepen van generaal Jourdan de vesting van Luxemburg, na een beleg van zeven maanden. Luxemburg werd, onder de Republiek en het Keizerrijk, het Departement Wouden (Département des Fôrets). De weerstand tegen de bezetter was zeer fel. De «knuppeloorlog» — *Klöppelkrieg* — werd in alle hevigheid gevoerd. Maar tegen de goed bewapende en georganiseerde Fransen maakten de boeren geen schijn van kans. Vier dagen na de val van Napoleon, op 15 april 1815, zette Luxemburg de deuren open voor de geallieerde troepen. Het land droeg nog de sporen van zijn lijdensweg. De abdijen van Orval en van Clairfontaine werden tijdens de eerste dagen van de Franse invasie in brand gestoken, de abdij van Echternach werd omgebouwd tot plateelbakkerij.

Op het Congres van Wenen beslisten de zegevierende mogendheden om weer een koninkrijk der Nederlanden te vormen, met de provincies van het noorden en het zuiden samen onder de scepter van Willem I van Oranje-Nassau. Maar Pruisen dwong ze ertoe een speciaal statuut te verlenen aan Luxemburg: enkele vorstendommen op het grondgebied van Nassau werden aan de koning van Pruisen geschonken en op basis van het compensatieprincipe ging het oude hertogdom Luxemburg, ondertussen verheven tot groothertogdom, als persoonlijk eigendom naar de koning der Nederlanden. Wel zou een Pruisisch leger van 4 000 man garnizoen houden in de burcht. De koning-groothertog Willem I bekommerde er zich niet om dat het groothertogdom theoretisch tot de Duitse Bond behoorde en beschouwde het als de achttiende provincie van zijn rijk. Vier Luxemburgse afgevaardigden zetelden trouwens in de Kamer bij de 55 vertegenwoordigers van de zuidelijke provincies. De bevolking toonde zich betrekkelijk tevreden over haar nieuwe lot en hield zich afzijdig van de grieven tegen het Huis van Oranje-Nassau. De beperking van de persvrijheid raakte haar niet: er was in Luxemburg maar één krant, die in het Frans publiceerde en weinig voor polemiek voelde. Daarentegen stuitte de aanwezigheid van de 4 000 Pruisen in de burcht iedereen tegen de borst, behalve dan de kleine handelaars.

Wellicht spoorde dit onder meer talrijke Luxemburgse patriotten aan om zich geestdriftig aan te sluiten bij de Belgische revolutie van 1830. De tijdelijke regering van de jonge Belgische staat verklaarde zonder aarzelen dat Luxemburg een integrerend deel was van België. Maar in 1831 kantte de Conferentie van Londen zich fel tegen deze hereniging. Het verdrag der XXIV Artikelen splitst Luxemburg in twee: het *Duitssprekende* deel (2 586 km²) werd toegekend aan Willem I als groothertog, het voornamelijk Waalse gedeelte (4 439 km²) ging naar België en werd de Belgische provincie Luxemburg. De Hollandse koning bleef er maar op hopen dat de situatie in zijn voordeel zou uitdraaien en weigerde zijn handtekening onder het verdrag te zetten. Resultaat : heel Luxemburg bleef acht jaar lang Belgisch. Op 14 maart 1838 moest de koning der Nederlanden er zich bij neerleggen dat België voorgoed was afgescheurd van het Huis van Oranje en aanvaardde eindelijk het scheidingsverdrag.

De deling van Luxemburg zoals het verdrag van de XXIV Artikelen bepaalde, werd zodoende definitief in 1839. Tot grote frustratie van de groothertogen met heimwee naar een verenigd hertogdom. Maar ook de Belgen betreurden het verlies van een inmiddels vertrouwd leven in gemeenschap.

De Europese omwentelingen van 1848 spaarden België, maar veroorzaakten wel deining in Holland. Willem II zag zich namelijk gedwongen om het volk een grondwet te geven, naar het voorbeeld van België. Zijn zoon Willem III meende dat de zaken van het groothertogdom maar moeilijk te beheren waren vanuit Den Haag. Hij vertrouwde het

bestuur — het «luitenantschap» — toe aan zijn broer Hendrik, een rechtvaardig man die rekening hield met de gevoelens van de Luxemburgse bevolking en meteen op handen werd gedragen.

De Franse keizer Napoleon III vergeleek Luxemburg met Savoie. Het was zijn grote droom om het te kopen van Willem III, die daar wel voor te vinden was en er 5 miljoen goudfranken voor vroeg. Maar het groothertogdom behoorde nog steeds tot de Duitse Bond en tot de Pruisische Unie, het *Zollverein*; bovendien had het verdrag der XXIV Artikelen geen einde gemaakt aan de aanwezigheid van een Pruisisch garnizoen in de vesting. Er moest dus onderhandeld met Bismarck, de kanselier van de koning van Pruisen. Deze had net Oostenrijk verslagen bij Sadowa en was niet echt bereid tot toegevingen: de onderhandelingen sleepten aan van november 1866 tot april 1867. Ook Willem III had de goedkeuring van Pruisen gevraagd. Toen dit verstek liet gaan en verklaarde dat de Belgische neutraliteit in zekere zin ook voor Luxemburg gold, was hij er niet meer zo happig op om te verkopen. Napoleon III was besluiteloos. Het vooruitzicht van een oorlog tussen Frankrijk en Pruisen dook op. Hij durfde er zich niet aan te wagen en dus stelde de Franse keizer voor om Luxemburg aan te hechten bij België, in ruil voor de regio's Philippeville en Mariembourg. De Belgische regering verzette zich uiteraard tegen deze combinatie die nergens op sloeg. Uiteindelijk ging Napoleon III akkoord met een internationale conferentie in Londen, die zou beslissen over de neutraliteit van het groothertogdom onder garantie van de Mogendheden, over de ontmanteling van het vestingwerk van de stad Luxemburg en het vertrek van het Pruisisch leger.

Bij de dood van Willem III in 1890, trad het familiepact dat de verschillende takken van de familie Nassau in 1783 sloten en dat werd opgenomen in de akten van het Congres van Wenen, in voege. Het groothertogdom Luxemburg, een erfgoed van de familie Nassau, ging naar Adolf van Nassau-Weilburg, wiens hertogdom ten noorden van de Main en ten oosten van de Rijn bij Pruisen was ingelijfd, met een compensatie van meer dan acht miljoen talers. Dit maakte een einde aan de Personele Unie van de Koning van Holland met de groothertog van Luxemburg.

De zoon van Adolf, Willem IV (r. 1904-1912) werd opgevolgd door zijn oudste dochter, Maria-Adelheid, die werd ingehaald als eerste vorstin die in het land was geboren.

Onder het bewind van Willem III en het luitenantschap van zijn broer, prins Hendrik, kende Luxemburg een periode van economische welvaart, dankzij de spoorwegnetten naar Thionville en Aarlen en later naar Trier. Zo was het niet langer afgezonderd. De invoer van cokes uit Luik maakte het mogelijk om af te stappen van hout en water als traditionele energiebronnen voor de gieterijen, voor de verwerking van het oölithisch erts dat de broeders Metz aan de grens met Frans Lotharingen ontdekten. De verwijdering van fosfor uit het erts, volgens het Thomas-procédé, was doorslaggevend: de productie van gietijzer in de fabrieken van Esch-sur-Alzette haalde in 1900 een miljoen ton, en anderhalf keer meer in 1913. De helft werd veredeld tot staal. De ijzer- en staalnijverheid, die overheerste in het economisch leven, leidde tot de ontwikkeling van de handhaving van middelgrote industrieën in sectoren van de mechanische bouwkunde, de leerlooierij, de handschoenmakerij, de brouwerij, aardewerk, en zeker ook de wijnbouw. Tegelijk trokken het rijke culturele erfgoed van het land en meer nog zijn zeer gevarieerde prachtige natuur, die de dichter Goethe en de schilder Turner zo bekoorden, meer en meer toeristen aan.

In 1914 respecteerden de Duitsers de Luxemburgse neutraliteit al evenmin als de Belgische. Zonder slag of stoot rukten ze beide landen binnen. Toch bleef de regering op post en draaide het raderwerk van de Staat verder. Ondanks de traditionele economische banden met Duitsland, was de bevolking openlijk vijandig tegen de bezetter. Zowat 1 500 jonge Luxemburgers namen dienst bij het Franse leger en bijna 300 bij het Belgische leger. Bij de bevrijding van het grondgebied, zetten groepen volksmenners de publieke opinie op tegen groothertogin Maria-Adelheid. Zij zou zogezegd de Duitsers eerder goedgezind zijn. De gemoederen raakten zo verhit dat Maria-Adelheid aftrad ten gunste van haar zuster Charlotte. Het voortbestaan van het groothertogdom Luxemburg stond op het spel. Fransen voerden verwoed maar subtiel propaganda ten voordele van een aansluiting bij de republiek. Van hun kant verenigden enkele Belgen zich in een Comité van Nationale Politiek en beriepen zich op de Geschiedenis die volgens hen in 1839 met de voeten was getreden. Beide partijen hadden echter een foute kijk op het diepgewortelde vaderlandsgevoel van de Luxemburgers en op hun onmiskenbare identiteit, zoals blijkt uit hun devies: *Mir wëlle bleiwe wat mir sin, «Wij willen blijven wie we zijn.»*

De wolken die zich samenpakten boven de Belgisch-Luxemburgse relaties verdwenen door de belofte van de Belgische koning Albert I om Charlotte onbeperkt te steunen. Op 28 september 1919 spreekt een volksraadpleging die de Luxemburgse regering organiseerde, zich met een verpletterende meerderheid uit ten gunste van groothertogin Charlotte, maar onder invloed van de Franse propaganda kozen de Luxemburgers meteen ook voor een economische unie met Frankrijk, en niet met België. De, totaal overbodige en onverantwoorde, handhaving van Franse garnizoenen, misnoegde de bevolking echter en, zoals te verwachten was, verzette de Britse regering zich tegen een Frans-Luxemburgse unie, in welke vorm ook. Daarbij vreesden de grote industriële groepen van Lotharingen de concurrentie van de Luxemburgse fabrieken op de Franse binnenlandse markt. De Belgisch-Luxemburgse Economische Unie (B.L.E.U.) werd opgericht op 1 mei 1921 en vanaf 1935 had de Belgische frank waarde in Luxemburg. De buitenlandse handel van de B.L.E.U. nam een vlucht die alle verwachtingen overtrof. Omdat beide landen elkaar zo goed aanvulden, werd de unie in 1938 al de grootste exporteur van staalproducten ter wereld. En Luxemburg werd de zetel van het internationaal staalkartel.

Op 10 mei 1940 werd Luxemburg, samen met België en Nederland, bezet en leed er zwaar onder dat de nazi's het land als Duits grondgebied beschouwden. Groothertogin Charlotte en haar regering kozen het pad van de ballingschap. *Gauleiter* Gustaf Simon had de handen vrij. Tot zijn grote woede verwierpen de Luxemburgers bij de volkstelling met vragenlijst van 10 oktober 1940 echter massaal de aansluiting bij het Reich. Reactie van de bezetter: vanaf 1942 werden twaalfduizend jonge mannen gedwongen om te strijden in een uniform en voor een zaak waar ze niets mee te maken hadden en 12 % van de bevolking werd weggevoerd. De bevrijding van het grondgebied was nog niet afgerond toen maarschalk von Rundstedt in december 1944 zijn verwoestend offensief inzette, dat het IIIde Amerikaanse leger van generaal Patton terugsloeg. Op 13 februari 1945 waren Vianden en Echternach eindelijk bevrijd en, op 14 april, keerde de groothertogin die was ondergedoken in Portugal en daarna in de Verenigde Staten, triomfantelijk terug naar haar hoofdstad.

Ondertussen hadden de Luxemburger Joseph Bech, de Belg Paul-Henri Spaak en de Nederlander E.N. van Kleffens op 14 september 1944 hun handtekening gezet onder de akkoorden voor de oprichting van de Benelux. Vanaf dat moment had Luxemburg, samen met zijn twee partners, actief deel aan de lange tocht naar de Europese eenmaking.

Meteen hernam de politieke activiteit weer haar traditionele gangetje, ook al ontstond er even een beweging die was geboren uit de Weerstand, de Unie van Luxemburgse Verzetsbewegingen (Unio'n). De oude partijen werden weer gevormd, op meer of minder nieuwe grondslagen: de christen-sociale partij die de meeste regeringsleiders leverde, internationale spelers zoals Joseph Bech, Pierre Werner, Jacques Santer en Jean-Claude Juncker; de socialistische arbeiderspartij die in de jaren 1969-1971 een scheuring kende onder de naam sociaal-democratische partij; de liberale partij die in de jaren zestig verjongde met de komst van persoonlijkheden zoals Gaston Thorn (die later de E.E.G.-Commissie in Brussel zal voorzitten) en Colette Flesch; de communistische partij die meer en meer in een al even nutteloze als onverbiddelijke positie gedreven wordt.

In de recente geschiedenis van de sociale betrekkingen in Luxemburg, merken C. Calmes en D. Bossaert op, was er maar zeer zelden sprake van stakingen. De inschakeling van overleg- en adviesorganen wist deze meestal te vermijden. Uiteraard wordt dit klimaat van sociale vrede bevorderd door de economische welvaart van Luxemburg. Deze wordt nog aangezwengeld door de omvang van de financiële sector — 178 banken — dankzij een fiscale wetgeving die kapitalen aantrekt. Het aanzienlijke belang van de banksector vormde ook een welkom tegenwicht voor de crisis van de jaren zeventig, die de Luxemburgse ijzer- en staalnijverheid, — de «ruggengraat van de economie» — toch ook in nauwe schoentjes bracht. De dynamiek in de sector bevorderde tevens structurele wijzigingen, zoals de uitbouw van de diensten, met name radio en televisie en telecommunicatie per satelliet. Van 1975 tot 1992 konden zich een honderdtal nieuwe grote en goed presterende bedrijven vestigen in Luxemburg.

De Luxemburgse vorsten doen hun grondwettelijk werk zonder zich te mengen in de politiek en zijn onpartijdig. «Het is pas met groothertogin Charlotte en dankzij haar», meent historicus Gilbert Trausch, «dat de dynastie van Nassau-Weilburg echt populair wordt. Haar lange regeringsperiode bewijst de invloed die een vorst kan hebben die regeert, maar niet bestuurt». In 1964 trad groothertogin Charlotte af ten gunste van haar zoon Jan die in 1953 in de echt was verbonden met prinses Josephine-Charlotte van België, dochter van koning Leopold III en koningin Astrid.

Hun oudste zoon, prins Henri, huwde op 14 februari 1981 Maria Teresa Mestre. In 1998 benoemde groothertog Jan Henri tot 'Luitenant-vertegenwoordiger' en op 7 oktober 2000 ruimde hij voor hem plaats op de troon. Het groothertogelijk paar heeft vier zonen en een dochter: de prinsen Guillaume, Felix, Louis, prinses Alexandra en prins Sebastien. De 276 600 Luxemburgers kunnen dus op beide oren slapen, het voortbestaan van de dynastie waar ze zo verknocht aan zijn, is verzekerd.

SAUF la Chiers à la frontière franco-belge, toutes les rivières qui zèbrent de leur charme le Luxembourg rejoignent la Moselle, directement ou après confluent. Nous suivrons leur cours, tantôt paisible, tantôt tumultueux, et traverserons chacune des régions géologiques bien distinctes qui composent le pays.

Suivre le cours des rivières, c'est aussi rencontrer et admirer un patrimoine culturel dont la variété le dispute à la richesse.

MIT Ausnahme der Korn an der belgisch-französischen Grenze fließen alle Flüsse, die Luxemburg so reizvoll durchziehen, direkt oder indirekt in die Mosel. Wir werden ihrem — mal ruhigen, mal lebhaften — Lauf folgen und die ganz unterschiedlichen geologischen Regionen, die das Land ausmachen, durchstreifen.

Wenn man dem Lauf der Flüsse folgt, kann man ein Kulturerbe entdecken und bewundern, dessen Vielfalt ebenso beeindruckend ist wie seine Fülle.

ALL the rivers that add so much charm to Luxembourg flow into the Moselle, either directly or after confluence, except for the Chiers on the Franco-Belgian frontier. We will follow their courses, sometime peaceful and sometimes turbulent, through each of the differing geological regions of the country.

By following the course of these rivers we will also encounter and admire a cultural heritage whose variety is as great as its richness.

BUITEN de Chiers aan de Frans-Belgische grens, monden alle rivieren die Luxemburg zoveel charme verlenen, uit in de Moezel, rechtstreeks of na samenvloeiing. Wij volgen hun nu eens vredige en dan weer stormachtige loop en doorkruisen zo stuk voor stuk de sterk onderscheiden geologische regio's die het land vormen.

Een tocht langs de rivieren voert ook naar een bewonderenswaardig cultureel erfgoed dat al even verscheiden als rijk is.

Voyage au pays de l'eau
Reise durch das Land des Wassers
Journey Through the River Lands
Tocht door het land van het water

Le lac du barrage de l'Our, un matin d'automne. Il arrive que, par chance, le brouillard nocturne se lève dès les premiers rayons d'un pâle soleil.

Der Our-Stausee an einem Herbstmorgen. Manchmal kann man beobachten, wie der Nachtnebel sich mit den ersten Strahlen einer bleichen Sonne hebt.

The lake behind the dam on the Our on an autumn morning, where sometimes the night mists begin to melt away when the first feeble rays of sunshine penetrate them.

Het stuwmeer van de Our op een herfstmorgen. Soms kan men zien hoe de nachtelijke nevel vanaf de eerste stralen van een zwakke zon optrekt.

Terres rouges,
aux sources de la Chiers et de l'Alzette

Land der roten Erde,
die Quellen von Korn und Alzette

Tout en prenant des directions opposées, la Chiers et l'Alzette prennent l'une et l'autre leur source au sein des terres ferrugineuses. L'exploitation intensive des gisements de minerai de fer appelé minette à partir du XIXe siècle transforma la vie rurale des habitants et, par l'afflux des ouvriers, provoqua le développement de petites agglomérations comme Lamadelaine et Rodange, au pied du Tëtelbierg.

Korn und Alzette fließen zwar in entgegengesetzte Richtungen, entspringen aber beide in eisenhaltiger Erde. Der intensive Abbau der Minette genannten Eisenerzvorkommen ab dem 19. Jh. verwandelte den Alltag der Einwohner und führte durch den Zustrom der Arbeiter zur Entstehung kleiner Siedlungen wie Lamadelaine und Rodange am Fuße des Tëtelbierg.

The Red Earth Country, source of the Chiers and the Alzette

Het land van de Rode Aarde, aan de bronnen van de Chiers en de Alzette

Although the Chiers and the Alzette flow in opposite directions they both rise in the heart of the iron ore region. Intensive exploitation of the deposits of iron ore called minette from the 19th century on transformed rural life and, with the influx of workers, led to the development of small towns such as Lamadelaine and Rodange at the foot of the Tëtelbierg.

Ze gaan een tegengestelde richting uit, maar de Chiers en de Alzette ontspringen allebei in de ijzerhoudende aarde. De intensieve ontginning van de ijzerertslagen, het zogenoemde minette, vanaf de 19de eeuw betekende een hele kentering in het landelijk leven van de bewoners en leidde, door de toestroom van de arbeiders, tot het ontstaan van kleine agglomeraties zoals Lamadelaine en Rodange aan de voet van de Tëtelbierg.

▲▶▶

Jadis entourée d'une enceinte fortifiée, **Esch-sur-Alzette** était devenue une bourgade rurale lorsque l'atteignit le boom industriel du XIXᵉ siècle. Sa population passa rapidement de 696 habitants à plus de 29 000. Cette brusque poussée démographique se situait à une époque où fleurissaient les styles architecturaux mis en œuvre dans la construction des demeures de la bourgeoisie. Plusieurs façades qui bordent la rue de l'Alzette (*double page suivante*) alternent le style éclectique — la façade de la maison Sichel (*ci-dessus*), ornée de guirlandes et fruits — avec les néo-gothique, néo-Renaissance, néo-baroque... La maison Meder (*à droite*), édifiée dans la rue Zénon Bernard par l'architecte Olivio Moïse pour un commerçant italien, révèle l'influence du style Art Nouveau par les grilles en fer forgé et les décors floraux de sa façade.

Das früher von einem Befestigungsgürtel umgebene **Esch-sur-Alzette** war zu einem ländlichen Marktflecken geworden, als es vom Industrieboom des 19. Jhs. erreicht wurde. Die Einwohnerzahl stieg rasch von 696 auf über 29.000. Dieser plötzliche demographische Schub kam zu einer Zeit, zu der die architektonischen Stile, die beim Bau der Wohnsitze des Bürgertums zum Einsatz kamen, eine Blütezeit erlebten. Bei mehreren Fassaden der rue de l'Azette (*folgende Doppelseite*) wechselt sich der eklektische Stil — die mit Girlanden und Früchten geschmückte Fassade des Sichel-Hauses (*oben*) — mit Neugotik, Neurenaissance und Neubarock... ab. Beim Meder-Haus (*rechts*), das Architekt Olivio Moïse in der rue Zénon Bernard für einen italienischen Händler gebaut hat, zeigt sich in den schmiedeeisernen Gittern und der Blumenverzierung der Fassade der Einfluss des Jugendstils.

Esch-sur-Alzette, formerly surrounded by fortifications, became a small rural town during the industrial boom of the 19th century, its population rapidly increasing from 696 inhabitants to more than 29,000. This rapid population increase took place during a period of architectural diversity in the building of middle-class housing. A number of façades lining the Rue de l'Alzette (*pages 46-47*) alternately present eclectic styles such as the façade of the Sichel house (*above*) decorated with garlands and fruit neighbor to neo-Gothic, neo-Renaissance and neo-baroque houses. The Meder house (*right*) built in Rue Zénon Bernard by the architect Olivio Moïse for an Italian businessman shows the influence of Art Nouveau in its wrought iron railings and the floral motifs on the façade.

Het eertijds omwalde **Esch-sur-Alzette** was uitgegroeid tot een plattelandsdorpje, toen de industriële boom er in de 19de eeuw kwam opzetten. De bevolking steeg al snel van 696 inwoners naar meer dan 29 000. Deze plotse demografische groei viel in een periode waarin de burgerij woningen in een prachtige architectuur liet bouwen. Een aantal gevels aan de rue de l'Alzette (*blz. 46-47*) wisselen een eclectische stijl — de gevel van het Sichel huis (*hierboven*), getooid met slingers en vruchten — af met neo-gotiek, neo-renaissance, neo-barok... Het Meder huis (*rechts*), dat architect Olivio Moïse in de rue Zénon Bernard bouwde voor een Italiaanse handelaar, weerspiegelt de invloed van de Art Nouveau in zijn hek van ijzersmeedwerk en de florale gevelversiering.

◄◄◄►

Vus depuis le sommet du **Prënzebierg**, les signes d'activité moderne contrastent avec la verdeur de la vallée où la Chiers et l'Alzette prennent leur source. Cet **ancien bassin minier**, qui s'étire sur une longueur d'une vingtaine de kilomètres, forme la frontière du grandduché avec le Luxembourg belge et la France. Les autorités luxembourgeoises l'ont aménagé en respectant et imposant les normes du paysage rural où alternent pâtures, vergers, bois de hêtres et de bouleaux.

La région, qui fut occupée par les Trévires dès le VIᵉ siècle avant Jésus-Christ, bénéficiait de la protection du proche oppidum du Tëtelbierg, ou mont Titus. Les Romains s'y installèrent par la suite, de même que sur le Prënzebierg où des milliers de monnaies gauloises ont été découvertes. Une route romaine mettait la région en communication avec l'importante ville d'Arlon.

Vom Gipfel des **Prënzebierg** aus gesehen, kontrastiert die moderne Industrie mit dem Grün des Tales, in dem Korn und Alzette entspringen. Dieses **ehemalige Kohlenbecken**, das sich auf einer Länge von rund zwanzig Kilometern erstreckt, bildet die Grenze zwischen dem Großherzogtum Luxemburg und der belgischen Provinz Luxemburg und Frankreich. Die luxemburgischen Behörden haben es unter Einhaltung und Auferlegung der Normen der ländlichen Landschaft gestaltet, bei der Weiden, Obstgärten sowie Buchen- und Birkenwälder dominieren.

Die ab dem 6. Jh. v. Chr. von den Treverern besiedelte Region profitierte vom Schutz des nahe gelegenen Oppidum Tëtelbierg (Titusberg), wo sich die Römer später ebenso wie auf dem Prënzebierg, wo Tausende gallischer Münzen entdeckt wurden, niederließen. Eine römische Straße verband die Region mit der bedeutenden Stadt Arlon.

Looking from the summit of the **Prënzebierg**, the signs of modern activity contrast with the verdant valley where the Chiers and the Alzette take their sources. This **ancient mining area** stretches for some twenty kilometres, forming the frontier of the Grand Duchy with the Belgian province of Luxembourg and with France. The Luxembourg authorities have developed it with respect, imposing the traditional norms of a rural countryside with alternating pastures, orchards and beech and birch woods.

The region, first settled by the Treveri from the VIth century BC, profited from the protection of the nearby oppidum of Tëtelbierg, or Mount Titus, later occupied by the Romans. Thousands of Gallic coins have been discovered here. A Roman road connected the region with the important town of Arlon.

Van de top van de **Prënzebierg** staan de tekens van de moderne activiteit in schril contrast met het groen van de vallei waar de Chiers en de Alzette ontspringen. Dit **oude mijnbekken**, dat zich uitstrekt over twintig kilometer, vormt de grens van het groothertogdom met Belgisch Luxemburg en Frankrijk. De Luxemburgse overheid richtte het in volgens de normen van het rurale landschap in een afwisseling van weiden, boomgaarden, berken- en beukenbossen.

De streek, waar de Treveri in de zesde eeuw vóór onze jaartelling neerstreken, genoot de bescherming van het nabije oppidum van de Tëtelbierg of Titusberg, waar Romeinen zich nadien vestigden, net als op de Prënzebierg waar duizenden Gallische muntstukken ontdekt werden. Een Romeinse heirbaan verbond de streek met de belangrijke stad Aarlen.

▲▶▶

La *minette*, ainsi appelée à cause de sa faible teneur en fer, entre 20 et 35 pour cent, était souvent extraite à ciel ouvert. C'était le cas au **Prënzebierg** que creusent encore des fronts de taille abrupts. L'épuisement progressif des gisements qui comptaient parmi les plus grands d'Europe et, surtout, le surcoût de l'exploitation de minerais moins riches que ceux que l'on pouvait importer du Brésil, de Suède et de Lorraine, entraînèrent la fermeture des mines au XXᵉ siècle. Et la nature reprit ses droits.

De nouveaux biotopes se sont développés à l'abri de réserve naturelles attentivement protégées, où sont aménagés des sentiers comme celui du «Giele Botter» sur le Prënzebierg.

Minette iron ore, so called because of its low iron content, between 20 and 35 percent, was often extracted in open-pit mines. Such is the case at **Prënzebierg**, still marked by the working faces. The progressive exhaustion of the deposits, once among the greatest in Europe and, above all, the elevated cost of working a mineral less rich in content than those available from Brazil, Sweden and Lorraine led to the closure of the mines in the 20th century and the reclamation of the terrain by nature.

New biotopes have developed in the shelter of the well-protected nature reserves with hiking paths such as the 'Giele Botter' on the Prënzebierg.

Die ihren Namen dem geringen Eisengehalt — zwischen 20 und 35 Prozent — verdankende Minette wurde häufig im Tagebau gewonnen. Dies war auch beim **Prënzebierg** der Fall, der noch heute von steilen Abbaustößen durchzogen wird. Die allmähliche Erschöpfung der Vorkommen, die zu den größten Europas zählten, und vor allem die Mehrkosten der Förderung von Erzen, die weniger stark erzhaltig waren als die, die man aus Brasilien, Schweden und Lothringen importieren konnte, führten zur Schließung der Bergwerke im 20. Jh. Und die Natur kam wieder zu ihrem Recht.

In sorgfältig geschützten Naturschutzgebieten haben sich neue Biotope entwickelt, in denen Wege wie der ,Giele Botter' auf dem Prënzebierg angelegt wurden.

Het typische ijzererts («minette» genoemd om het geringe ijzergehalte, tussen 20 en 35 percent) werd vaak in bovengrondse mijnen gewonnen. Zo ook op de **Prënzebierg** met zijn steile werkfronten als stille getuigen. De geleidelijke uitputting van de lagen, die tot de grootste in Europa behoorden, en vooral de hoge kosten voor de ontginning van erts dat minder rijk was dan wat kon ingevoerd uit Brazilië, Zweden en Lotharingen, leidden tot de sluiting van de mijnen in de 20ste eeuw. En de natuur eiste haar rechten weer op.

Nieuwe biotopen ontwikkelden zich in de schaduw van waakzaam beschermde natuurreservaten, met aangelegde paden zoals de 'Giele Botter' op de Prënzebierg.

Luxembourg,
où l'Alzette rencontre la Pétrusse

Luxemburg,
wo die Alzette die Petrusse trifft

Une première grande enceinte protégeait la ville de Luxembourg depuis la fin du XII⁰ siècle. Elle fut agrandie et renforcée au cours du XIV⁰, mais c'est au cours des XVI⁰ et XVII⁰ siècles que le vaste réseau des fortifications fit de Luxembourg la «Gibraltar du nord». Après avoir été conquise par l'armée de Louis XIV en 1684, elle fut l'objet de gigantesques travaux dirigés par Vauban. Ce qui subsiste des murailles et des tours, et surtout les casemates, demeure impressionnant. La place de la Constitution occupe l'emplacement de la plate-forme du grand bastion Beck. Un accès aux casemates de la Pétrusse, de l'époque espagnole, y a d'ailleurs été aménagé.

Seit Ende des 12. Jhs. wurde die Stadt Luxemburg durch eine erste große Ringmauer geschützt. Im Laufe des 14. Jhs. wurde sie vergrößert und verstärkt, und im 16. und 17. Jh. ließ das große Festungsnetz Luxemburg zum „Gibraltar des Nordens" werden. Nach der Eroberung durch die Armee von Ludwig XIV im Jahre 1684 war es Gegenstand gigantischer Arbeiten unter der Leitung von Vauban. Die Überreste der Mauern und Türme und vor allem der Kasematten sind noch heute beeindruckend. Der Platz der Verfassung liegt am Orte der Plattform der großen Beck-Bastion. Zu spanischer Zeit wurde dort ein Zugang zu den Kasematten der Petrusse angelegt.

Luxembourg, where the Alzette and the Petrusse meet

Luxemburg, waar de Alzette de Petrusse tegenkomt

The first great walls protecting the city of Luxembourg date to the end of the 12th century. They were enlarged and strengthened during the 14th century but it was during the 16th and 17th centuries that the great network of its fortifications made Luxembourg the "Gibraltar of the North". When it was conquered by the army of Louis XIV in 1684 the huge defensive works were undertaken by Vauban. That which remains of the walls and towers and the casemates in particular is very impressive. Constitution Square occupies the area of the platform of the great bastion of Beck. An entrance to the casemates of the Petrusse, dating from the Spanish period, has been constructed there.

Een eerste grote omwalling beschermde de stad Luxemburg vanaf het einde van de 12de eeuw. Deze werd vergroot en versterkt in de loop van de 14de eeuw, maar pas in de 16de en 17de eeuw maakte het uitgebreide netwerk van versterkingen van Luxemburg het «Gibraltar van het noorden». Na de inname door het leger van Lodewijk XIV in 1684 werd ze grondig herbouwd, onder leiding van Vauban. Wat nog rest van de walmuren en van de torens, en vooral van de kazematten, is werkelijk indrukwekkend. De huidige place de la Constitution ligt op het vroegere platform van het grote Beck-bastion. Er werd trouwens een toegang aangelegd tot de kazematten van de Petrusse uit de Spaanse tijd.

Le démantèlement de la forteresse commença en 1867; il se termina en 1883. Le carcan qui empêchait le tissu urbain de s'étendre avait définitivement disparu. Il s'ensuivit aussitôt une expansion de la ville hors des anciens remparts, vers l'ouest, le nord-ouest puis vers le sud. Il fallut dès lors prévoir des ponts pour relier les différents quartiers : la ville en comptera 110. Construit entre 1899 et 1903, le pont Adolphe fut conçu pour assurer la jonction du centre-ville avec la nouvelle gare située à l'est sur le plateau Bourbon. L'ouvrage d'art, considéré comme audacieux pour l'époque, enjambe la **vallée de la Pétrusse** à quarante mètres de hauteur.

À gauche
À l'extrémité du plateau Bourbon, le beffroi du siège de la Caisse d'Épargne domine la vallée de la Pétrusse.

Das Schleifen der Festung begann 1867 und endete 1883. Die Zwangsjacke, die eine Ausbreitung der Stadt verhinderte, war damit endgültig verschwunden. Es folgte eine Ausbreitung der Stadt über die ehemalige Befestigungsanlage hinaus nach Westen, Nordwesten und schließlich nach Süden. Nun mussten Brücken gebaut werden, um die einzelnen Viertel miteinander zu verbinden: die Stadt sollte 110 dieser Bauwerke zählen. Die zwischen 1899 und 1903 errichtete Adolf-Brücke sollte das Stadtzentrum mit dem im Osten auf dem Bourbon-Plateau gelegenen neuen Bahnhof verbinden. Das für die Zeit kühne Bauwerk überspannt das **Petrusse-Tal** in vierzig Metern Höhe.

Links
Am Ende des Bourbon-Plateaus überragt der Belfried des Sitzes der Sparkasse das Petrusse-Tal.

Demolition of the fortress began in 1867 and was finished in 1883. The walls that prevented the expansion of the city were gone for good. The city then spread out beyond the old ramparts to the west, northwest and later the south. It was necessary to build bridges to link the various new areas and the city would construct 110. The Adolph Bridge, built between 1899 and 1903, was designed to connect the centre of the city to the new railway station to the east on the Bourbon plateau. This elegant structure, considered as audacious at that epoch, bestrides the **valley of the Petrusse** at the height of forty meters.

Left

The belfry of the seat of the Savings Bank at the far side of the Bourbon plateau dominates the valley of the Petrusse.

De ontmanteling van het bolwerk begon in 1867 om te eindigen in 1883. Het keurslijf dat een rem zette op de uitbouw van het stedelijk weefsel was eens en voor al verdwenen. De stad breidde meteen uit tot voorbij de vroegere walmuren, naar het westen, het noordwesten en vervolgens zuidwaarts. Er moesten dus ook bruggen komen om de wijken met elkaar te verbinden: de stad telt er 110. De pont Adolphe, die werd gebouwd tussen 1899 en 1903, werd ontworpen om het stadscentrum aan te sluiten op het nieuwe station ten oosten, op het 'plateau Bourbon'. Het kunstwerk, dat voor die tijd gewaagd werd geacht, overspant de **vallei van de Petrusse** op een hoogte van veertig meter.

Links

Aan het uiteinde van het plateau Bourbon, torent het belfort van de Stadsspaarbank uit boven de vallei van de Petrusse.

Laissé pratiquement à l'abandon au cours du XIXᵉ siècle et au début du XXᵉ, le **Grund** a été rénové dans les années 1980-1990 et réanimé par la présence de bistrots très fréquentés par les citadins.

Der Vorort Grund, der im 19. und Anfang des 20. Jhs. nahezu sich selbst überlassen war, wurde in den 80er und 90er Jahren des 20. Jhs. renoviert und durch bei den Städtern sehr beliebte Bistros neu belebt.

The **Grund** was nearly abandoned during the 19th and early 20th centuries but was restored in the '80s and '90s and revived by the many bars well patronized by the city dwellers.

Grund werd van de 19de tot het begin van de 20ste eeuw praktisch aan haar lot overgelaten, maar in de jaren 1980-1990 volledig gerenoveerd en tal van bistro's die druk worden bezocht door de stedelingen brengen er volop leven in de brouwerij.

Après son confluent avec la Pétrusse, l'Alzette parcourt le **faubourg du Grund** au pied de la Vieille Ville et des fortifications. Au moyen âge déjà, le quartier était peuplé de nombreux artisans et commerçants qui s'étaient fixés le long de l'Alzette. Ils livraient le produit de leur travail aux habitants de la ville haute où était concentrée la vie politique, économique et religieuse de Luxembourg.

Downstream from the confluence with the Petrusse, the Alzette flows through the **Grund suburb** at the foot of the fortified Old Town. In the Middle Ages the Grund was already inhabited by numerous artisans and merchants established along the Alzette. They delivered the fruits of their labour to those dwelling in the upper town where the political, economic and religious life of Luxembourg was concentrated.

Nach dem Zusammenfluss mit der Petrusse durchquert die Alzette den **Vorort Grund** am Fuße der Altstadt und der Befestigungsanlagen. Bereits im Mittelalter war dieses Viertel von zahlreichen Handwerkern und Händlern, die sich entlang der Alzette niedergelassen hatten, bevölkert. Sie lieferten die Erzeugnisse ihrer Arbeit an die Einwohner der Oberstadt, in der sich das politische, wirtschaftliche und religiöse Leben Luxemburgs abspielte.

De Alzette vloeit samen met de Petrusse en loopt dan door de **voorstad Grund**, aan de voet van de Oude Stad en de versterkingen. In de Middeleeuwen al was de wijk bevolkt met tal van ambachtslieden en handelaars die zich langs de Alzette hadden gevestigd. Ze leverden het product van hun arbeid aan de bewoners van de bovenstad waar het politieke, economische en religieuze leven van Luxemburg zich afspeelde.

Ci-dessus et page de droite

Vus depuis la «Corniche» et les fortifications, **la vieille ville et le Grund**, d'où pointe le clocher de l'église Saint-Jean (1698-1705), ont séduit les voyageurs les plus illustres. «On trouve ici, écrivit Goethe, tant de grandeur et de charme, tant de gravité et de grâce qu'on aurait désiré que le peintre Poussin eût mis son talent au service de ces espaces.» Aussitôt après avoir acquis en 963 l'éperon rocheux du **Bock**, le comte Sigefroi y édifia un château fort dominant la vallée de l'Alzette sur trois côtés et protégé par une série de tours. Les fouilles entreprises en 1963 et en 1992 ont permis de mettre en valeur les vestiges découverts.

Double page suivante

Non loin du château, sur le plateau où fut édifiée la **Vieille Ville** aux alentours de l'église Saint-Michel, se trouvait la basse cour. Elle groupait les communs et les habitations des serviteurs du comte.

Oben und rechte Seite

Von der „Corniche" und den Festungsanlagen aus gesehen, haben **die Altstadt und der Grund**, in dem der Kirchturm der Johannes-Kirche (1698-1705) emporragt, die berühmtesten Reisenden in ihren Bann gezogen. „Hier findet sich", schrieb Goethe, „soviel Größe mit Anmut, soviel Ernst mit Lieblichkeit verbunden, dass wohl zu wünschen wäre, Poussin hätte sein herrliches Talent in solchen Räumen betätigt". Unmittelbar nach der Eroberung des **Bock**-Felsvorsprungs ließ Graf Sigfrid dort ein Kastell errichten, das das Alzette-Tal auf drei Seiten beherrschte und von einer Reihe von Türmen geschützt wurde. Nach den 1963 und 1992 durchgeführten Ausgrabungen konnten die entdeckten Überreste zur Geltung gebracht werden.

Folgende Doppelseite

Nicht weit vom Schloss entfernt befand sich auf dem Plateau, auf dem die **Altstadt** um die St.-Michaelskirche herum erbaut worden war, der Unterhof mit den Wirtschaftsgebäuden und den Wohngebäuden der Diener des Grafen.

Above and page right

The old city and the Grund, whence rises the steeple of Saint John's church (1698-1705), seen from the ledge — the "corniche" — with its fortifications, has charmed many famous visitors. "One finds here," wrote Goethe, "such grandeur and charm, so much dignity and grace that one might desire the artist Poussin, with all his talent to depict this panorama." Soon after Count Sigefroid acquired the rocky spur of the **Bock** he built a castle dominating the Alzette valley on three sides and protected by a series of towers. Archaeological digs between 1963 and 1992 have uncovered imposing vestiges.

Pages 66-67

Not far from the castle on the plateau where the **Old Town** was built around Saint Michael's church was the farmyard with the outbuildings and the dwellings of the Count's servants.

Hierboven en rechter pagina

De Alzette loopt door **Grund** waar de klokkentoren van de Saint-Jean kerk (1698-1705) priemt. Het uitzicht dat de «corniche» en de vestingen op de oude stad bieden, wist de meest illustere reizigers te bekoren. «Hier vindt men», schreef Goethe, «zoveel grandeur en charme, zoveel ernst en sierlijkheid dat men zou wensen dat de schilder Poussin zijn talent ten dienste van deze ruimtes had gesteld.» Meteen na de verovering van de rots van de **Bock** in 963, trok graaf Siegfried er een versterkt kasteel op dat aan drie kanten uitkeek over de vallei van de Alzette en door een reeks torens werd beschermd. De opgravingen in 1963 en in 1992 legden de resten bloot.

Pagina's 66-67

In de buurt van het kasteel, op het plateau waar de **Oude Stad** rond de Saint-Michel kerk werd opgetrokken, bevond zich het neerhof. Dit groepeerde de bijgebouwen en de woningen van de dienaars van de graaf.

La **cathédrale Notre-Dame** est l'ancienne église du collège fondé par les Jésuites peu après leur arrivée à Luxembourg. L'architecte en était le frère Jean de Block qui conçut les plans d'une remarquable église-halle de style gothique tardif, solennellement consacrée en 1621 par l'évêque électeur de Trèves. Le sanctuaire, élevé au rang de cathédrale en 1874, fut agrandi de 1935 à 1936 du côté sud. Une tour et le transept furent ajoutés.

Dans la crypte, un escalier conduit au mausolée de la famille grand-ducale. Depuis 1946, les restes de Jean l'Aveugle, comte de Luxembourg et roi de Bohême mort à la bataille de Crécy en 1346, y reposent dans un sarcophage du XVIᵉ siècle provenant de l'ancienne abbaye de Neumünster.

Die **Kathedrale Unserer Lieben Frau** ist die ehemalige Kirche des von den Jesuiten kurz nach ihrer Ankunft in Luxemburg gegründeten Kollegiums. Der Architekt war Bruder Johannes de Block, der die Pläne einer bemerkenswerten Hallenkirche im spätgotischen Stil entwarf. 1621 wurde sie feierlich vom Kurfürstbischof von Trier geweiht. Das Heiligtum, das im Jahre 1874 in den Rang einer Kathedrale erhoben wurde, wurde 1935 und 1936 auf der Südseite vergrößert. Ein Turm und das Querschiff wurden hinzugefügt.

In der Krypta führt eine Treppe zum Mausoleum der großherzoglichen Familie. Seit 1946 liegen die sterblichen Überreste des Grafen von Luxemburg und Königs von Böhmen, Johannes der Blinde, der 1346 in der Schlacht von Crécy gestorben ist, in einem Sarkophag aus dem 16. Jh., der aus der ehemaligen Abtei von Neumünster stammt.

The **Cathedral of Our Lady** was formerly the church of a college founded by the Jesuits shortly after their arrival in Luxembourg. The Bishop-Elector of Trier solemnly consecrated it in 1621. The architect was Brother Jean de Block who designed a remarkable hall church in the Late Gothic style. The sanctuary, raised to the rank of Cathedral in 1874, was enlarged in 1935-36 on the south side. A tower and transept were added.

A staircase in the crypt leads to the mausoleum of the Grand Ducal family. In 1946 the remains of John the Blind, Count of Luxembourg and King of Bohemia who died at the Battle of Crécy in 1346 were placed in a 16th century sarcophagus coming from the former Abbey of Neumünster.

De **Notre-Dame kathedraal** is de oude kerk van het college dat de Jezuïeten kort na hun aankomst in Luxemburg stichtten. Ze werd plechtig ingehuldigd in 1621 door de keurbisschop van Trier. De architect was broeder Jean de Block die de plans ontwierp voor een opmerkelijke hallenkerk in laat-gotische stijl. Het heiligdom, dat in 1874 tot de rang van kathedraal werd verheven, werd van 1935 tot 1936 aan de zuidkant uitgebreid. Een toren en het transept werden toegevoegd.

In de crypte leidt een trap naar het mausoleum van de groothertogelijke familie. Sinds 1946 rusten de overblijfselen van Jan de Blinde, graaf van Luxemburg en koning van Bohemen, die sneuvelde in de veldslag van Crécy in 1346, in een sarcofaag uit de 16de eeuw, die afkomstig is van de oude abdij van Neumünster.

Le **palais grand-ducal** a été érigé en plusieurs étapes. La partie la plus ancienne, à gauche, a été construite de 1572 à 1573 sur ordre du gouverneur Pierre-Ernest de Mansfeld. Elle est de style Renaissance mais le décor des frises qui séparent les étages et les fenêtres montre une évidente influence hispano-mauresque. Le bâtiment, qui servit longtemps d'hôtel de ville, fut agrandi au XVIIIᵉ siècle par une construction qui disparut au profit d'un édifice de style Renaissance française, réalisé à l'initiative du grand-duc Adolphe (au centre et à droite).

Depuis 1892, le palais est la résidence officielle de la famille grand-ducale. Dans une salle du premier étage sont reçus, pour la remise de leurs lettres de créance, les ambassadeurs, envoyés extraordinaires et ministres plénipotentiaires accrédités au Luxembourg.

Der **großherzogliche Palast** wurde in mehreren Etappen errichtet. Der älteste Teil (links) wurde von 1572 bis 1573 auf Befehl des Gouverneurs Peter-Ernst von Mansfeld gebaut. Er ist im Renaissance-Stil gehalten, aber die Verzierung der Frise, die die Etagen und Fenster trennen, zeigt einen deutlichen spanisch-maurischen Einfluss. Das Gebäude diente lange Zeit als Rathaus und wurde im 18. Jh. durch ein Bauwerk vergrößert, das dann zugunsten eines auf Initiative des Großherzogs Adolf errichteten Gebäudes im französischen Renaissancestil verschwunden ist.

Seit 1892 dient der Palast der großherzoglichen Familie als offizielle Residenz. In einem Saal in der ersten Etage werden die in Luxemburg akkreditierten Botschafter, Gesandten und Sondergesandten zur Überreichung Ihrer Beglaubigungsschreiben empfangen.

The **Grand Ducal Palace** was built in several stages. The oldest part, to the left, was built in 1572-73 by command of Governor Peter Ernst von Mansfeld. The style is Renaissance but the décor of the friezes separating the stories and the windows show a marked Hispano-Moorish influence. For a long period the building served as the Town Hall and was enlarged in the 18th century by an addition that was later replaced by another construction in the French Renaissance style by Grand Duke Adolph (centre and right).

The palace has served as the residence of the Grand Ducal family since 1892. In a reception room on the first floor ambassadors, special emissaries and plenipotentiaries accredited to Luxembourg are received to present their credentials.

Het **groothertogelijk paleis** werd in fasen gebouwd. Het oudste gedeelte (links) dateert van 1572-1573 en werd gebouwd op bevel van Peter Ernest van Mansfeld, gouverneur van het hertogdom Luxemburg. Het is in renaissancestijl, maar uit het decor van de friezen tussen de verdiepingen en de ramen spreekt duidelijk een Spaans-Moorse invloed. Het gebouwde diende lange tijd als stadhuis en werd in de 18de eeuw vergroot met een gebouw dat nadien weer plaats maakte voor een pand in Franse renaissancestijl, op initiatief van groothertog Adolf.

Sinds 1892 dient het paleis als officiële residentie van de groothertogelijke familie. In een zaal op de eerste verdieping worden de geloofsbrieven in ontvangst genomen van de ambassadeurs, buitengewone gezanten en gevolmachtigd ministers die in Luxemburg geaccrediteerd zijn.

▲▶
Comme le rappelle l'inscription d'un cartouche sur la façade, le bâtiment du **ministère des Affaires étrangères** était jadis un refuge de l'abbaye Saint-Maximin de Trèves; il abritait moines et moniales en temps de guerre. Reconstruit en 1751 dans le style noble Louis XV, il servit à partir de 1839 de logement aux autorités militaires prussiennes. Ce n'est qu'en 1867, après le départ enfin obtenu de la garnison étrangère, que le gouvernement luxembourgeois put s'y installer.

Ayant abandonné sa neutralité après la seconde guerre mondiale, le Luxembourg a mené une politique extérieure très active dans le cadre de l'O.N.U. et de ses institutions spécialisées, du Benelux et de la Communauté européenne. Le rôle significatif qu'il joue en usant de son droit de codécision dans les structures de l'Union européenne dépasse de loin la taille du pays.

Wie die Inschrift einer Kartusche auf der Fassade zeigt, war das Gebäude des **Außenministeriums** früher ein Refugium der Abtei Sankt Maximin von Trier. In Kriegszeiten beherbergte es Mönche und Nonnen. 1751 im vornehmen Stil von Ludwig XV wieder aufgebaut, diente es ab 1839 den preußischen Militärbehörden als Unterkunft. Erst 1867 konnte sich die luxemburgische Regierung nach dem endlich erreichten Abzug der ausländischen Garnison dort niederlassen.

Nach Aufgabe seiner Neutralität nach dem zweiten Weltkrieg hat Luxemburg im Rahmen der Vereinten Nationen und seiner besonderen Institutionen des Benelux und der Europäischen Gemeinschaft eine sehr aktive Außenpolitik betrieben. Die wichtige Rolle, die das Land durch Nutzung seines Mitentscheidungsrechts in der Europäischen Union spielt, übersteigt bei Weitem die Größe des Landes.

An ornamental tablet on the façade of the **Foreign Affairs Ministry** recalls that the building was once a refuge for the monks and cloistered nuns of the Abbey of Saint Maximin of Trier during time of war. Rebuilt in 1751 in the grandiose Louis XV style it served as lodgings for the Prussian military command from 1839 on. It was only after their departure in 1867 that the Luxembourg government was able to take it over.

Luxembourg abandoned its neutrality after World War II and has led a very active role in external policies within the United Nations and its various institutions, and in the Benelux and the European Community. The role that it plays in the framework of the European Union, thanks to the right of co-decision, is significantly greater than the size of the country.

Zoals het opschrift in een cartouche op de gevel meldt, was het gebouw van het **ministerie van Buitenlandse Zaken** eertijds een toevluchtsoord van de Sint-Maximinusabdij van Trier; het ving monniken en slotzusters op in tijden van oorlog. Na de heropbouw in 1751 in adellijke Lodewijk XV-stijl, diende het vanaf 1839 als onderkomen voor de Pruisische legeraanvoerders. Pas in 1867, toen het buitenlandse garnizoen eindelijk vertrok, kon de Luxemburgse regering er intrekken.

Luxemburg had zijn neutraliteit opgegeven na de tweede wereldoorlog en voerde een zeer actief buitenlands beleid in het kader van de Verenigde Naties en de gespecialiseerde instellingen, van de Benelux en van de Europese Gemeenschap. Zijn doorslaggevende rol die het speelt met zijn medebeslissingsrecht in de structuren van de Europese Unie overtreft ruim het formaat van het land.

Contiguë à la cathédrale, la «**maison de Bourgogne**» fut occupée dès le XVᵉ siècle, notamment par le gouverneur représentant l'empereur Maximilien d'Autriche. Sa tour d'escalier, à laquelle on accède par une porte sommée d'un linteau en accolade, dénote la transition du style gothique à celui de la Renaissance. L'édifice abrite les bureaux du Ministre d'État, le chef du gouvernement luxembourgeois.

Das an die Kathedrale angrenzende **Burgunderhaus** wurde seit dem 15. Jh. genutzt, vor allem von dem Gouverneur, der Kaiser Maximilian von Österreich vertrat. Sein Treppenturm, über den man durch eine Tür mit geschweiftem Sturz gelangt, zeugt vom Übergang vom gotischen Stil zum Renaissance-Stil. Das Gebäude beherbergt die Büros des Staatsministers, der Leiter der luxemburgischen Regierung ist.

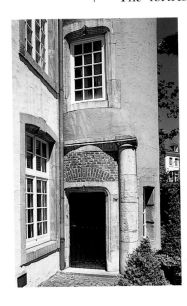

The **House of Burgundy**, adjacent to the Cathedral, has been occupied since the 15th century, most notably by the Governor representing Maximilian of Austria. The staircase turret, which is entered by a door crowned with a Gothic lintel, shows the transition from the Gothic style to that of the Renaissance. The offices of the Minister of State, head of the Luxembourg government, are situated in this building.

Naast de kathedraal ligt het **Bourgondisch huis** dat vanaf de 15de eeuw werd bewoond, onder meer door de gouverneur die keizer Maximiliaan van Oostenrijk vertegenwoordigde. Zijn traptoren, die toegankelijk is via een poort met een gotische latei, geeft de overgang aan van de gotiek naar de renaissance. Het gebouw huisvest de kantoren van de Minister van Staat, het hoofd van de Luxemburgse regering.

La forteresse de Luxembourg, qui comprenait plus de 40 000 mètres-carrés de casernes, ne fut pas totalement détruite lors de son démantèlement en 1867. Outre le labyrinthe de ses casemates, il subsiste un certain nombre de tours, tourelles et autres tronçons des ouvrages de défense. Le «**mur de Wenceslas**» date du XVᵉ siècle; il a donné son nom au pont de pierre sur l'Alzette.

Die Festung von Luxemburg, die über 40.000 Quadratmeter Kasernen umfasste, wurde bei ihrer Schleifung 1867 nicht vollständig zerstört. Neben dem Labyrinth ihrer Kasematten sind einige Türme, Türmchen und andere Elemente der Verteidigungsbauwerke erhalten. Die **Befestigungsmauer von Wenzel** stammt aus dem 15. Jh. und stand Pate für die Steinbrücke über die Alzette.

The fortress of Luxembourg with its more than 40,000 square meters of barracks, was not completely destroyed when it was demolished in 1867. As well as the labyrinth of blockhouses a certain number of towers, turrets and bits of defensive works still remain. The 'Wenceslas wall', dating from the 15th century, has given its name to the stone bridge over the Alzette.

Het fort van Luxemburg, dat meer dan 40 000 vierkante meter kazernes bevatte, werd niet volledig vernield tijdens de sloop van 1867. Buiten de doolhof van zijn kazematten, rest er nog een heel aantal torens, torentjes en andere stukken verdedigingswerken. De **muur van Wenceslaus** dateert uit de 15de eeuw; hij gaf zijn naam aan de stenen brug over de Alzette.

L'Alzette, de Luxembourg à la Sûre

Die Alzette, von Luxemburg bis zur Sauer

Avant de quitter Luxembourg et couler vers Mersch, Colmar-Berg, Ettelbrück pour rejoindre la Sûre, l'Alzette sinue au pied du plateau du Kirchberg qui a reçu une destinée européenne. La Cour de Justice de l'Union européenne y siège et, tout proche, le bâtiment du centre européen peut accueillir 890 invités dans sa grande salle. À gauche, à l'arrière-plan, se profile la pyramide vitrée du nouveau musée d'art moderne Grand-Duc Jean. Dans la vallée, à Clausen, la rivière arrose une brasserie.

Ehe die Alzette Luxemburg in Richtung Mersch, Colmar-Berg und Ettelbrück verlässt, um dort in die Sauer zu fließen, schlängelt sie sich am Fuße des Kirchberg-Plateaus entlang, das europäische Bedeutung erlangt hat. Hier tagt der Gerichtshof der Europäischen Gemeinschaften. Das ganz in der Nähe gelegene Gebäude des Europa-Zentrums bietet in seinem großen Saal Platz für 890 Gäste. Links im Hintergrund sieht man die gläserne Pyramide des Museums für Moderne Kunst Großherzog Jean. In dem im Tal gelegenen Clausen versorgt der Fluss eine Brauerei mit Wasser.

The Alzette, from Luxembourg to the Sûre

De Alzette, van Luxemburg naar de Sûre

Before leaving Luxembourg on its journey towards Mersch, Colmar-Berg, Ettelbrück and its junction with the Sûre, the Alzette winds around the foot of the Kirchberg plateau, now the site of several European institutions. The Court of Justice of the European Communities has its seat here and the Council of Europe building nearby can welcome 890 delegates in the Great Hall. In the background, to the left, rises the glass pyramid of the Grand Duke Jean Museum of Modern Art. In the valley the river flows past a brewery in Clausen.

Voor de Alzette Luxemburg verlaat en de richting van Mersch, Colmar-Berg en Ettelbrück kiest, om zich bij de Sûre te voegen, kronkelt hij aan de voet van het Plateau van Kirchberg dat een Europese bestemming kreeg. De zetel van het Hof van Justitie van de Europese Unie is er gevestigd en vlakbij kan het gebouw van het Europees centrum in zijn grote zaal 890 genodigden onthalen. Links, op de achtergrond, verrijst de glaspiramide van het Museum voor Hedendaagse Kunst "Grand-Duc Jean". In de vallei, in Clausen, vloeit de rivier handig langs een brouwerij.

◄▲

Grossie des eaux de ses affluents l'Eisch et la Mamer, l'Alzette arrose la petite ville de **Mersch** où ont été dégagés les substructures et le vaste bassin d'une villa romaine du Ier siècle.

Sur une hauteur, le donjon carré fut édifié en 1232 par le chevalier Théodoric Ier de Mersch, vassal de la comtesse Ermesinde. Détruit par les Français en 1453, le château fut reconstruit en 1585. Il subit deux nouveaux sièges destructeurs au cours du XVIIe siècle; sa reconstruction dans sa forme actuelle date du siècle suivant auquel appartient le portail flanqué de deux échauguettes. Il fut restauré en 1975.

Nach dem Zufluss von Eisch und Mamer erreicht die Alzette das Städtchen **Mersch**, wo der Untergrund und das große Becken einer römischen Villa aus dem 1. Jh. freigelegt worden sind.

Der auf einer Anhöhe liegende Bergfried wurde 1232 von Ritter Theodoric I von Mersch, einem Vasallen der Gräfin Ermesinde, gebaut. Das 1453 von den Franzosen zerstörte Schloss wurde 1585 wieder aufgebaut. Im 17. Jh. erlebte es zwei weitere zerstörerische Belagerungen. Sein Wiederaufbau in seiner derzeitigen Form erfolgte im 18. Jh., in dem das von zwei Warten flankierte Portal hinzukam. Es wurde 1975 restauriert.

Swollen by the waters of its tributaries the Eisch and the Mamer, the Alzette waters the little town of **Mersch** where the substructures of the huge pool of a Roman villa of the 1st century have been uncovered.

The knight Theodoric I of Mersch, vassal of Countess Ermesinde, built a square keep on the heights in 1232. It was destroyed by the French in 1453 and rebuilt in 1585. It suffered two more destructive sieges during the 17th century. It was rebuilt in its present form during the following century with its portal flanked by two watchtowers. It was restored in 1975.

De Alzette krijgt het gezelschap van zijn zijrivieren de Eisch en de Mamer, om dan samen door de kleine stad **Mersch** te trekken. Daar werden de substructuren en het uitgestrekte bassin van een Romeinse villa uit de eerste eeuw blootgelegd.

In 1232 trok ridder Theodoricus I van Mersch, vazal van gravin Ermesinde, er op een hoogte een vierkante donjon op. Het kasteel werd in 1453 vernield door de Fransen en in 1585 heropgebouwd. Het onderging nog twee verwoestende belegeringen in de loop van de 17de eeuw; de heropbouw in zijn huidige vorm dateert uit de volgende eeuw, met het portaal dat geflankeerd is door twee wachttorentjes. Het werd gerestaureerd in 1975.

Le vallon de la Mamer, un affluent de l'Alzette, où s'élève l'imposant donjon du château de **Schoenfels** est cerné, à l'est, par la file de rochers dans lesquels de nombreuses cavernes ont été creusées. Sur la route dite des sept châteaux, celui de Schoenfels servait d'avantposte au château de Mersch. En 1684, il fut rasé par les Français qui n'épargnèrent que le donjon. Celui-ci reçut au XIXᵉ siècle une toiture néo-gothique y compris deux pignons à redents et quatre échauguettes. Adjonction quelque peu insolite mais qui accompagnait une opportune restauration de l'édifice.

Die Talmulde des Alzette-Zuflusses Mamer, in der sich der eindrucksvolle Bergfried des Schlosses von **Schoenfels** erhebt, ist im Osten von einer Reihe von Felsen, in die zahlreiche Höhlen gegraben sind, umgeben. Im sogenannten Tal der sieben Schlösser diente das Schloss von Schoenfels als Vorposten für das Schloss von Mersch. 1684 wurde es von den Franzosen, die nur den Bergfried verschonten, geschleift. Letzterer erhielt im 19. Jh. ein neugotisches Dach mit zwei Shed-Giebeln und vier Warten. Diese Ergänzung ist ein wenig ungewöhnlich, ging jedoch mit einer sinnvollen Restaurierung des Gebäudes einher.

The imposing keep of the castle of **Schoenfels** dominates the little valley of the Mamer, a tributary of the Alzette, that is ringed on the east by a series of huge rocks hollowed out by many caverns. Schoenfels, on the so-called route of seven castles, was an outpost of Mersch castle. The French razed it in 1684, sparing only the keep which received a neo-Gothic roof with two toothed gables and four watchtowers in the 19th century. These additions were a little odd but formed part of a timely restoration.

De vallei van de Mamer, een zijrivier van de Alzette, waar de indrukwekkende donjon van het kasteel van **Schoenfels** verrijst, wordt aan de oostkant ingesloten door de rij rotsen waarin tal van grotten uitgehouwen werden. Op de zogenaamde 'route van de zeven kastelen' diende het slot van Schoenfels als voorpost voor het kasteel van Mersch. In 1684 maakten de Fransen het met de grond gelijk, enkel de donjon bleef gespaard. Deze kreeg in de 19de eeuw een neogotisch dak, met twee tandvormige rondelen en vier wachttorentjes. Dit lijkt wel een vrij vreemde toevoeging, maar past perfect in de restauratie van het gebouw.

Depuis leur château, les petits seigneurs féodaux se livraient à la chasse, leur divertissement favori. Assez intransigeante pour ses sujets, elle méprisait le luxe ostentatoire. Pendant ce temps-là, les manants vivaient chichement de l'agriculture dans leurs villages. À **Keispelt**, le Service des sites et monuments s'est efforcé de restaurer les maisons rurales. L'aspect idyllique a définitivement effacé le souvenir des misères d'antan.

Von ihrem Schloss aus widmeten sich die kleinen Feudalherren ihrer Lieblingsbeschäftigung, der Jagd. Sie waren gegenüber ihren Untertanen recht unnachgiebig und lehnten großtuerischen Luxus ab. Während dessen lebten die Bauern kärglich in ihren Dörfern von der Landwirtschaft. In **Keispelt** bemühte sich das staatliche Amt für Denkmalpflege um die Restaurierung der ländlichen Häuser. Das idyllische Aussehen hat die Erinnerung an das frühere Elend endgültig ausgelöscht.

The small feudal lords amused themselves by hunting around their castles. Ruling their subjects with an iron hand, they disdained ostentation and luxury. The villains subsisted on what their village could grow. At **Keispelt** the Service of Sites and Monuments has restored the rural dwellings. Their idyllic aspect has erased the memories of the miserable existence of yesteryears.

Vanuit hun kasteel, gaven de lagere feodale heren zich over aan de jacht, hun geliefde tijdverdrijf. Ze waren weinig toegeeflijk voor hun onderdanen en minachtten opzichtige luxe. In die tijd overleefden de dorpsbewoners amper van de landbouw in hun dorpen. In **Keispelt** spande de Dienst Landschappen en Monumenten zich in om de plattelandshuisjes te restaureren. Het schilderachtige uitzicht verwijst de herinnering aan een ellendige tijd definitief naar het verleden.

La vallée de l'Eisch, une petite rivière qui se jette dans l'Alzette, traverse une partie du Gutland qui a gardé son caractère traditionnel et parfois sauvage. À quelques kilomètres de Schoenfels, le château de **Hollenfels** a été construit au XIIIe siècle sur un promontoire creusé d'une grotte, ce qui lui donna son nom de *rocher creux*. Sa tour atteint 40 mètres de hauteur et sa muraille 23 mètres. Une aile d'habitation fut ajoutée au XVIIIe siècle. Elle abrite aujourd'hui un centre d'écologie et une auberge de jeunesse.

Das Tal der Eisch, eines kleinen Flusses, der in die Alzette fließt, durchquert einen Teil von Gutland, der seinen traditionellen und zum Teil unberührten Charakter gewahrt hat. Einige Kilometer von Schoenfels entfernt wurde das Schloss von **Hollenfels** im 13. Jh. auf einer aus einer Grotte ausgehöhlten Landspitze gebaut, was seinen Namen erklärt. Sein Turm ist 40 hoch, während seine Mauer eine Höhe von 23 Metern erreicht. Im 18. Jh. wurde ein Wohnflügel hinzugefügt, der heute ein Zentrum für Ökologie und eine Jugendherberge beherbergt.

The valley of the Eisch, a little river that flows into the Alzette, crosses a part of the Gutland that has kept its traditional and sometimes wild character. A few kilometres from Schoenfels is the castle of **Hollenfels**, built in the 13th century on a promontory hollowed out by a cave which gives it its name of "hollow rock". Its tower rises to 40 meters and its wall to 23 meters. A dwelling wing was added in the 18th century. Now it serves as an ecological centre and youth hostel.

De vallei van de Eisch, een kleine rivier die zich in de Alzette stort, loopt door een deel van het Gutland (Goedland) dat zijn traditionele en soms zelfs woeste karakter bewaarde. Op enkele kilometers van Schoenfels is het kasteel van **Hollenfels** te vinden. Dit werd in de 13de eeuw opgetrokken op een met een grot ingehouwen voorgebergte, wat het de naam *holle rots* gaf. Zijn toren is wel 40 meter hoog en zijn muur 23 meter. In de 18de eeuw kwam er een woonvleugel bij. Vandaag is er een ecologisch centrum en een jeugdherberg gehuisvest.

◄◄

S'étirant dans la vallée de l'Eisch, le village de **Septfontaines** est accroché au flanc boisé du versant. Ses maisons aux façades enduites de peinture rose sont groupées au pied des murailles de la forteresse du XIIᵉ siècle qui releva longtemps de l'abbaye d'Echternach. Une tour gothique ronde lui fut adjointe au XVᵉ siècle et une autre, de style Renaissance, au XVIIᵉ. Un incendie ravagea le château à la fin du XVIIIᵉ siècle.

Un petit cimetière entoure l'église Saint-Michel édifiée en 1316. Il est jalonné par les stations sculptées d'un chemin de croix daté de 1737.

The village of **Septfontaines** on the wooded flank of a slope stretches along the Eisch valley. The pink-washed houses are grouped around the walls of the 12th century fortress that belonged for a long time to the abbey of Echternach. A round Gothic tower was added to it in the 15th century and another in the Renaissance style was added at the end of the 18th century.

A small cemetery surrounds the church of Saint Michael built in 1316. It is studded with sculpted statues of the Stations of the Cross, dating from 1737.

Das sich im Eisch-Tal erstreckende Dorf **Septfontaines** schmiegt sich an die bewaldete Seite des Hangs. Die rosa gestrichenen Häuser liegen am Fuße der Mauern der Festung aus dem 12. Jh., die lange Zeit der Abtei von Echternach unterstand. Im 15. Jh. kam ein runder gotischer Turm hinzu und im 17. Jh. ein weiterer im Renaissance-Stil. Ende des 18. Jhs. wurde das Schloss von einem Brand heimgesucht.

Ein kleiner Friedhof umgibt die Sankt Michael-Kirche, die 1316 errichtet worden ist. Sie ist von mit Reliefen verzierten Stationen eines Kreuzweges aus dem Jahre 1737 umgeben.

Het dorp **Septfontaines** strekt zich uit in de vallei van de Eisch en ligt genesteld aan de beboste flank van de helling. Zijn in roze verf gestoken gevels staan verzameld aan de voet van de omwalling van het fort uit de 12de eeuw dat lange tijd toebehoorde aan de abdij van Echternach. Een ronde gotische toren werd toegevoegd in de 15de eeuw en een tweede, in renaissancestijl, in de 17de. Een brand legde het kasteel in de as op het einde van de 18de eeuw.

Een klein kerkhof omgeeft de Saint-Michel kerk die in 1316 werd opgetrokken. Het is afgebakend met de gebeeldhouwde staties van een kruisweg uit 1737.

▲◄

L'église Saint-Remi (1748) de **Koerich** est le premier édifice religieux baroque construit au Luxembourg. Dans le chœur, le maître-autel sculpté en bois de chêne et polychromé, est animé d'un mouvement ascensionnel triomphal. Au centre, il conjugue la vie de la Vierge Marie depuis l'Annonciation par l'Ange Gabriel jusqu'à l'Assomption. Sur les côtés, saint Remi s'apprête à baptiser Clovis, et saint Nicolas à ressusciter les enfants dans le saloir.

Le portail, entre deux pilastres aux chapiteaux corinthiens, est surmonté de niches que peuplent les statues de Notre Dame, saint Remi et sainte Lucie.

Die Sankt Remigiuskirche (1748) von **Koerich** ist das erste in Luxemburg errichtete barocke religiöse Gebäude. Im Chor wird der aus Eichenholz geschnitzte mehrfarbige Hauptaltar durch eine triumphal aufsteigende Bewegung belebt. In der Mitte wird das Leben der Jungfrau Maria von der Verkündigung durch den Engel Gabriel bis zur Himmelfahrt gezeigt. Auf den Seiten sieht man den Heiligen Remigius bei der Taufe von Chlodwig und den Heiligen Nikolaus bei der Wiederbelebung der Kinder im Pökelfass.

Über dem Portal zwischen zwei Pilastern mit korinthischen Kapitellen befinden sich Nischen mit Statuen von Unserer Lieben Frau, dem Heiligen Remigius und der Heiligen Luzia.

The church of Saint Remi (1748) of **Koerich** was the first baroque religious building constructed in Luxembourg. The polychrome oak high altar in the choir rises in a triumphant ascension. In the centre it depicts the life of the Virgin Mary from the Annunciation by the Archangel Gabriel to the Assumption. On the sides, Saint Remi prepares to baptize Clovis and Saint Nicholas is reviving the children in the pickle barrel.

Two pilasters with Corinthian capitals surround the portal surmounted by niches containing statues of Our Lady, Saint Remi and Saint Lucy.

De Saint-Remi kerk (1748) van **Koerich** is het eerste religieuze barokgebouw dat in Luxemburg werd gebouwd. Het eikenhouten polychrome hoofdaltaar in het koor behoort tot de fraaiste van het land. Het verhaalt in het midden het leven van de Maagd Maria van de Aankondiging door de engel Gabriël tot de Tenhemelopneming. Aan de zijkant maakt de heilige Remigius zich op om Clovis te dopen en is Sint Nikolaas klaar om de kinderen in het pekelvat weer tot leven te wekken.

Het portaal, tussen twee pilasters met Corinthisch kroonwerk in, draagt nissen met de beelden van Onze-Lieve-Vrouw, de heilige Remigius en de heilige Lucia.

Au milieu des bois, entre les vallées de l'Eisch et de l'Attert, le charme de **Saeul** est rehaussé par quelques fermes et maisons anciennes, restaurées par des citadins ou aménagées en restaurants, où se déploient toutes les nuances du rouge ou du rose. Cette couleur provenait à l'origine de la terre ferrugineuse mélangée à la chaux.

La nef centrale de l'église, de style roman tardif, date du XIIIᵉ siècle. Les bas-côtés ont été accolés au cours du XVIIIᵉ siècle. Le village n'étant pas protégé par un château, en temps de guerre les habitants se réfugiaient dans le grenier aménagé au-dessus du chœur roman de l'église, où subsiste une cheminée de pierre.

Mitten im Wald zwischen den Tälern von Eisch und Attert wird der Charme von **Saeul** durch einige ehemalige Bauernhöfe und Häuser gesteigert, die von Städtern restauriert oder zu Restaurants umgebaut wurden und alle Schattierungen von rot und rosa aufweisen. Diese Farbe stammte ursprünglich von der mit Kalk gemischten eisenhaltigen Erde.

Das Hauptschiff der spätromanischen Kirche stammt aus dem 13. Jh. Die Seitenschiffe sind im 18. Jh. hinzugekommen. Da das Dorf nicht durch ein Schloss geschützt wurde, flüchteten sich die Einwohner in Kriegszeiten in den über dem romanischen Chor der Kirche eingerichteten Dachboden, in dem ein Steinkamin erhalten ist.

The charm of **Saeul**, situated in the middle of the forest between the valleys of the Eisch and the Attert, is enhanced by some farms and old houses, restored by the citizens or converted into restaurants, painted in tones varying from pink to red. The local ferruginous earth mixed with lime provides these tints.

The central nave of the Late Romanesque church dates from the 13th century. The side aisles were added during the 18th century. Since the village was not protected by a castle, the inhabitants would seek refuge in the loft above the Romanesque choir of the church during periods of war. A stone chimney still exists there.

Temidden van de bossen, tussen de valleien van de Eisch en van de Attert krijgt de charme van **Saeul** nog een extra toets met enkele oude hoeves en woningen die stedelingen restaureerden of tot restaurant ombouwden in een hele schakering van rood of roze. Deze kleur is oorspronkelijk afkomstig van de ijzerhoudende aarde in een mengeling met kalk.

De hoofdbeuk van de kerk, in laat-romaanse stijl, dateert uit de 13de eeuw. De zijbeuken kwamen er pas vijf eeuwen later, in de loop van de 18de eeuw, bij. Het dorp werd niet beschermd door een kasteel en dus zochten de inwoners een toevlucht in de ingerichte zolder boven het romaanse koor van de kerk, waar nog een stenen schoorsteen te zien is.

À **Colmar-Berg**, où l'Attert rejoint l'Alzette, le souvenir s'est perdu du château fort dont les origines remontaient au XVᵉ siècle. Sur ses murs de base, Guillaume II, roi de Hollande et grand-duc de Luxembourg, fit entreprendre en 1845 la construction d'une résidence dans le style néo-gothique alors à la mode. Les travaux furent poursuivis entre 1907 et 1911. Entourés d'un grand parc, les bâtiments d'habitation et de réception comportent près de deux cents pièces. Lorsque le drapeau luxembourgeois flotte au sommet du donjon de soixante-cinq mètres de hauteur, chacun sait que le grand-duc est présent.

L'usine de pneu Goodyear s'est implantée à Colmar en 1951. Elle emploie plusieurs milliers de personnes et s'inscrit dans la politique de diversification économique du pays.

In **Colmar-Berg**, wo der Fluss Attert in die Alzette fließt, hat sich die Erinnerung an die auf das 15. Jh. zurückgehende Burg verloren. Auf ihren Grundmauern ließ der König von Holland und Großherzog von Luxemburg, Wilhelm II, 1845 eine Residenz in dem damals modernen neugotischen Stil errichten. Die Arbeiten wurden von 1907 bis 1911 fortgesetzt. Die von einem großen Park umgebenen Wohn- und Empfangsgebäude umfassen nahezu zweihundert Räume. Wenn die luxemburgische Fahne in 65 Metern Höhe auf dem Bergfried flattert, wissen alle, dass der Großherzog anwesend ist.

1951 hat sich die Reifenfirma Goodyear in Colmar niedergelassen. Sie beschäftigt mehrere Tausend Mitarbeiter und ist Teil der Politik zugunsten einer wirtschaftlichen Diversifizierung des Landes.

No one at **Colmar-Berg**, where the Attert joins the Alzette, remembers the old 15th century fortress that once stood there. In 1845 William II, King of the Netherlands and Grand Duke of Luxembourg, began the construction on the base of its walls of a residence in the fashionable neo-Gothic style of the period. More work was done between 1907 and 1911. The dwelling and reception buildings, surrounded by a large park, contain nearly two hundred rooms. When the Luxembourg flag flies from the top of the sixty-five meter high keep the Grand Duke is in residence.

A Goodyear tire factory was set up in Colmar in 1951. Employing several thousand workers, it is part of the economic diversification policy of the country.

In **Colmar-Berg** waar de Attert samenvloeit met de Alzette, bleef maar weinig over van de vesting die tot de 15de eeuw teruggaat. In 1845 gaf Willem II, koning der Nederlanden en groothertog van Luxemburg, de opdracht om op de steunmuren een residentie te bouwen in de neo-gotische stijl die toen erg in trek was. De werkzaamheden liepen verder tussen 1907 en 1911. De woon- en ontvangstgebouwen waren omrand door een groot park en bevatten zowat tweehonderd vertrekken. Als aan de top van de vijfenzestig meter hoge donjon de Luxemburgse vlag wappert, weet iedereen dat de groothertog er vertoeft.

In 1951 vestigde de bandenfabriek Goodyear zich in Colmar. Deze stelt enkele duizenden personeelsleden tewerk en kadert in het beleid van economische diversifiëring van het land.

▲▶

Les curiosités géologiques s'accumulent aux alentours immédiats du petit village de Nommern, arrosé par le Nommerbaach, petit affluent de l'Alzette. Au sud-ouest, dans la forêt, les masses rocheuses des **Nommerlayen** prennent des formes tourmentées, quelquefois fantasmagoriques. Tantôt leurs strates persistantes s'allongent en couches horizontales, tantôt ils se dressent, creusés, évoquant la gueule d'un dragon.

In unmittelbarer Nähe des kleinen Dorfes Nommern, durch das der Nommerbaach, ein kleiner Zufluss der Alzette fließt, häufen sich die geologischen Sehenswürdigkeiten. Im südwestlich gelegenen Wald zeigen die **Nommerlayen**-Felsmassen zerklüftete, zuweilen bizarre Formen. Mal ziehen sich ihre bleibenden Schichten in die Horizontale, mal stehen die ausgehöhlten Felsen aufrecht und erinnern an das Maul eines Drachen.

Geological curiosities abound in the immediate vicinity of the small village of Nommern, watered by the Nommerbaach, a little tributary of the Alzette. In the forest to the southwest the rocky massifs of **Nommerlayen** present tortured, fantastic shapes. Sometimes their sedimentary strata lie in horizontal layers and sometimes they rise, hollowed out and resemble the maw of a dragon.

De geologische bezienswaardigheden stapelen zich op in de onmiddellijke omgeving van het dorpje Nommern, waar de Nommerbaach, een bijriviertje van de Alzette, stroomt. In het zuidwestelijk gelegen bos nemen de rotsmassa's van **Nommerlayen** grillige en soms wat bizarre vormen aan. De ene keer strekken hun hardnekkige strata zich uit in horizontale lagen en dan richten ze zich uitgehold weer op en doen ze denken aan de muil van een draak.

92

◄◄
Au nord-est de **Nommern**, dans un vieux bois de chênes, les rochers du site de **la Lock** présentent d'innombrables rainures dues au polissage des silex. Les hommes du néolithique les taillaient pour en faire des pointes de flèches, des grattoirs, des perçoirs ainsi que des couteaux tranchants. Il est vrai que le village est aux portes du Müllerthal habité dès l'âge de la pierre.

Im Nordosten von **Nommern** weisen die in einem alten Eichengehölz liegenden **Lock**-Felsen unzählige Rillen auf, die vom Schleifen der Feuersteine herrühren. Die Menschen des Neolithikums haben sie behauen, um daraus Pfeilspitzen, Kratzer, Bohrer sowie scharfe Messer herzustellen. Das Dorf liegt am Eingang des bereits in der Steinzeit bewohnten Müllerthals.

To the northeast of **Nommern**, in an old oak wood, the rocks of the site of **la Lock** present innumerable grooves due to the polishing of flints. Neolithic man worked them in order to make arrowheads, scrapers and awls as well as daggers. The village lies at the gates of the Müllerthal, inhabited since the Stone Age.

Ten noordoosten van **Nommern**, in een oud eikenbos, vertonen de rotsen van **La Lock** ontelbare inkervingen die door het slijpen van vuurstenen ontstaan zijn. De mens uit het neolithisch tijdperk bewerkten deze stenen om er pijlpunten, schrapers, boren en scherpe messen van te maken. Dit dorp ligt dan ook aan de poort van het Müllerthal dat al vanaf de steentijd bewoond werd.

Au confluent de la Wark et de l'Alzette, s'appuyant sur les derniers contreforts de l'Oesling, **Ettelbruck** a cruellement souffert des bombardements pendant l'offensive allemande de von Rundstedt. Une statue du général Patton rappelle d'ailleurs le rôle libérateur de la IIIe Armée américaine. Seules demeuraient intactes quelques maisons anciennes et l'église néoromane. Mais la ville n'a pas tardé à renaître de ses ruines et à renouer avec une vie intense. Outre le musée Patton, elle présente depuis 1982 un musée consacré à la sauvegarde du patrimoine culturel de la région.

Das am Zusammenfluss von Wark und Alzette auf den letzten Ausläufern des Ösling gelegene **Ettelbrück** hat sehr unter den Bombardements während der deutschen Offensive von Rundstedts gelitten. Eine Statue von General Patton erinnert an die Befreiung durch die 3. amerikanische Armee. Es sind nur einige alte Häuser und die neuromanische Kirche erhalten. Aber die Stadt erstand bald wieder von ihren Ruinen auf und entwickelte ein reges Leben. Neben dem Patton-Museum besitzt sie seit 1982 auch ein Museum, das dem Erhalt des Kulturerbes der Region gewidmet ist.

Ettelbrück, at the confluence of the Wark and the Alzette, rests on the outlying spurs of the Oesling. It suffered grievously from shelling during the German offensive under von Rundstedt. A statue of General Patton celebrates the liberation by the American Third Army. Only a few houses and the neo-Romanesque church remained intact. The town quickly arose from its ruins and recommenced its intense activity. Besides the Patton Museum there is also a museum devoted to the cultural heritage of the region, founded in 1982.

Aan de samenvloeiing van de Wark en van de Alzette, vlijt **Ettelbrück** zich tegen de laatste uitlopers van de Oesling. De stad had het *zwaar* te verduren tijdens de bombardementen van het Duitse von Rundstedtoffensief. Een beeld van generaal Patton herinnert trouwens aan de bevrijdende rol van het IIIde Amerikaans leger. Alleen enkele oude huizen en de neo-romaanse kerk hielden stand. Maar de stad talmde niet om uit haar as te verrijzen en weer bij een bruisend leven aan te knopen. Naast het Patton museum is er sinds 1982 ook een museum dat gewijd is aan het cultureel erfgoed van de streek.

De la Sûre à l'Our, l'Oesling mystérieux

Von der Sauer zur Our, das geheimnisvolle Ösling

Grossie par les eaux de ses affluents, l'Alzette se jette dans la Sûre non loin d'Ettelbrück. Nous entrons ensuite dans cette partie du massif de l'Ardenne-Eifel que les Luxembourgeois appellent Oesling ou Eislek, un plateau constitué d'ardoise et de grès formé il y a plus de 370 millions d'années. Délimité à l'est par l'Our, il englobe environ un tiers du territoire du grand-duché de Luxembourg et comporte le point le plus élevé du pays avec ses 558,80 mètres au dessus du niveau de la mer.

In der Nähe von Ettelbrück fließt die vom Wasser ihrer Zuflüsse vergrößerte Alzette in die Sauer. Anschließend gelangen wir in den Teil des Ardennen-Eifel-Massivs, den die Luxemburger Ösling nennen: ein vor über 370 Millionen Jahren entstandenes Plateau aus Schiefer und Sandstein. Das im Osten von der Our begrenzte Gebiet umfasst rund ein Drittel des Gebiets des Großherzogtums Luxemburg und weist den bei 558,80 Metern über dem Meeresspiegel gelegenen höchsten

From the Sûre to the Our, the mysterious Oesling
Van de Sûre naar de Our, de raadselachtige Oesling

Swollen by the waters of its tributaries, the Alzette flows into the Sûre not far from Ettlebrück. We are now entering into the part of the Ardennes-Eifel that is called the Oesling in Luxembourg, a plateau made up of slate and sandstone formed more than 370 million years ago. Bordered on the east by the Our, it constitutes about a third of the territory of the Grand Duchy of Luxembourg and has the highest point in the country at 558.80 Sûters above sea level.

Onderweg dikt de Alzette aan met zijn zijrivieren en stort zich dan in de Sûre, op een boogscheut van Ettelbrück. Dan betreden wij dat deel van het massief van de Ardennen-Eifel dat de Luxemburgers Oesling of Eislek noemen, een plateau van leisteen en zandsteen dat meer dan 370 miljoen jaren geleden gevormd werd. Oostwaarts is het begrensd door de Our en het beslaat ongeveer een derde van het grondgebied van het groothertogdom Luxemburg. Hier is ook het hoogste punt van het land te vinden, op 558,80 meter boven de zeespiegel.

Pages 98 à 103

La Sûre qui prend sa source en Belgique traverse l'Oesling, où elle est rejointe par l'Our avant de se jeter dans la Moselle.

Haute de 48 mètres, la muraille d'un barrage réalisé en 1960 et 1961 a transformé, sur une vingtaine de kilomètres, le cours de la rivière en un lac de 380 hectares. Sa profondeur moyenne est de 16 mètres et sa contenance est de 60 millions de mètres-cubes. Il fournit essentiellement de l'eau potable mais, en hiver, une petite centrale hydroélectrique produit un apport énergétique.

Une partie du **lac de la Haute-Sûre** constitue un paradis pour les nageurs et les plongeurs, les amateurs de planche à voile et les pêcheurs. À l'entours, des sentiers bien balisés permettent la découverte du très beau parc naturel de la Haute-Sûre.

Seiten 98 bis 103

Die in Belgien entspringende Sauer durchfließt das Öesling und nimmt dort die Our auf, ehe sie in die Mosel fließt.

Die 48 Meter hohe Mauer eines 1960 und 1961 gebauten Staudamms hat den Flusslauf auf einer Strecke von zwanzig Kilometern in einen 380 Hektar großen See verwandelt. Er ist durchschnittlich 16 Meter tief und hat einen Inhalt von 60 Millionen Kubikmetern. Er liefert vor allem Trinkwasser, aber im Winter erzeugt ein kleines Wasserkraftwerk zusätzlich Energie.

Ein Teil des **Sees der oberen Sauer** ist ein Paradies für Schwimmer und Taucher, Surfer und Fischer. In der Umgebung kann man auf gut beschilderten Wegen den sehr schönen Naturpark Obere Sauer entdecken.

Pages 98 to 103

The Sûre takes its source in Belgium and then crosses the Oesling where it is joined by the Our before flowing into the Moselle.

The 48-meter high wall of a dam built in 1960-61 has changed over some twenty kilometres the course of the river into a 380-hectare lake. Its average depth is 16 meters and its capacity is 60 million cubic meters. Basically it furnishes drinking water but in winter a small hydroelectric station furnishes backup power.

Part of the **Haute Sûre Lake** is a paradise for swimmers and divers, sailboarders and fishers. Well-marked paths in the surrounding area run through the very beautiful Nature Park of the Haute Sûre.

Pagina's 98 tot 103

De Sûre die in België ontspringt, loopt door de Oesling, waar hij het gezelschap krijgt van de Our om daarna in de Moezel op te gaan.

De dammuur van 48 meter, die in 1960 en 1961 werd uitgevoerd, veranderde over een twintigtal kilometers de loop van de rivier in een meer van 380 hectare. De gemiddelde diepte bedraagt er 16 meter, voor een inhoud van 60 miljoen kubieke meter. Hij levert vooral drinkwater, maar tijdens de winter produceert een kleine waterkrachtcentrale ook extra energie.

Een deel van het **meer van de Boven-Sûre** is een waar paradijs voor zwemmers en duikers, windsurfers en vissers. In de omgeving voeren prima bewegwijzerde paden naar het zeer mooie natuurpark van de Boven-Sûre.

Cette double page ainsi que la suivante

En aval de la digue principale du lac, **Esch-sur-Sûre** fut le siège d'une seigneurie fondée au Xe siècle. Ce dont témoignent le château, les vestiges des fortifications médiévales et la grosse tour de guet érigée au XVe siècle.

Le village est parcouru de ruelles étroites et escarpées, bordées de maisons bourgeoises. Depuis les hauteurs des flancs boisés, elle apparaît littéralement enlacée par une boucle de la rivière.

This double page and the following double page

Downstream from the main dike of the lake lies **Esch-sur-Sûre**, the seat of a seigneury founded in the 10th century. The castle, remains of the mediaeval fortifications and the sturdy watchtower erected in the 15th century are still extant.

The village is crisscrossed with narrow and steep streets bordered by substantial houses. Seen from the heights of the wooded slopes, Esch-sur-Sûre seems to be completely clasped by a bend in the river.

Diese und die folgende Doppelseite

Das unterhalb des Hauptdeichs des Sees gelegene **Esch-an-der-Sauer** war der Sitz einer im 10. Jh. gegründeten Lehnsherrschaft. Davon zeugen das Schloss, die Überreste der mittelalterlichen Befestigungsanlagen und der dicke Wachturm aus dem 15. Jh.

Der Marktflecken wird von engen und steilen Gassen durchzogen, an denen bürgerliche Häuser liegen. Von den Höhen der bewaldeten Abhänge gesehen scheint er von einer Windung des Flusses umschlungen zu werden.

Deze dubbele pagina en ook de volgende

Stroomafwaarts van de hoofddijk van het meer ligt **Esch-sur-Sûre**, eertijds de zetel van een heerlijkheid in de 10de eeuw gesticht. Daarvan getuigen nog het kasteel, de resten van de middeleeuwse versterking en de grote uitkijktoren uit de 15de eeuw.

Het dorp is een doolhof van smalle, steile straatjes met burgerwoningen. Van op de hoogtes van de beboste flanken lijkt het letterlijk omhelsd door een lus van de rivier.

▲◄

Au creux d'un vallon boisé, non loin de la route de Wahl à Martelange, se cache le hameau de **Rindschleiden**; ses maisons se comptent sur les doigts d'une main. L'église Saint-Wilibrord a gardé des vestiges de l'époque romane : le clocher et des éléments de l'abside. Le chœur à chevet plat est du XVᵉ siècle, ses trois nefs sont d'après 1535. Un exceptionnel ensemble de fresques, découvert en 1952, orne les voûtes. Elles représentent une multitude de scènes bibliques, de saints et de personnages royaux, notamment les évangélistes Mathieu et Jean, saint Georges terrassant le dragon, le baptême du Christ, le couronnement de la Vierge. Les chapiteaux romans des deux colonnes soutenant les retombées de la voûte sont historiés de figures symboliques et allégoriques.

In einer bewaldeten Talmulde, nicht weit von der Straße von Wahl nach Martelange entfernt, versteckt sich der Weiler **Rindschleiden**. Seine Häuser sind an den Händen einer Hand abzuzählen. Die Sankt Willibrord-Kirche zeigt Überreste der romanischen Epoche: Glockenturm und Elemente der Absis. Der Chor mit flacher Absis stammt aus dem 15. Jh., die drei Kirchenschiffe aus der Zeit nach 1535. Die Gewölbe werden von einer außergewöhnlichen, 1952 entdeckten Freskensammlung geschmückt. Sie stellen eine Vielzahl von biblischen Szenen, Heiligen und königlichen Personen, insbesondere die Evangelisten Matthäus und Johannes, den Heiligen Georg, der den Drachen überwältigt, die Taufe Christi und die Krönung der Heiligen Jungfrau dar. Die romanischen Kapitelle der beiden Säulen, die das Gewölbe stützen, sind mit symbolischen und allegorischen Figuren verziert.

The hamlet of **Rindschleiden** lies hidden at the bottom of a wooded glen not far from the road from Wahl to Martelange. The houses can be counted on the fingers of one hand. The village church of Saint Willibrord still has vestiges of the Romanesque period such as the bell tower and parts of the apse. The choir with its flat chevet and the three naves date from after 1535. Exceptionally fine frescoes discovered in 1952 decorate the vaults. They present a multitude of biblical scenes, saints and royal persons as well as the Evangelists Matthew and John. Saint George slays the dragon and the Virgin is crowned. The Romanesque capitals of the two columns supporting the springing of the vault are historied with symbolic and allegoric figures.

In het hart van een bosrijke vallei, niet ver van de weg van Wahl naar Martelange ligt het gehucht **Rindschleiden** verscholen. Zijn huizen zijn op één hand te tellen. De kerk van de heilige Willibrord huisvest nog resten uit de romaanse tijd: de klokkentoren en elementen van de absis. Het koor met een vlakke afsluiting dateert uit de 15de eeuw, zijn drie beuken kwamen er na 1535 bij. Een uitzonderlijk ensemble van fresco's dat in 1952 werd ontdekt, siert de gewelven. Ze tonen een hele reeks bijbelse taferelen, heiligen en koninklijke figuren, onder meer de evangelisten Matteus en Jan, Sint Joris die de draak verslaat, het doopsel van Christus, de kroning van de heilige Maagd. De romaanse kapitelen van de twee zuilen die de aanzetten van het gewelf ondersteunen, zijn getooid met symbolische en allegorische figuren.

Après avoir serpenté gracieusement dans une vallée bordée d'étroites prairies et encerclée de collines boisées, la Wiltz se jette dans la Clerve à **Kautenbach**, village de quelque deux cents habitants. Le plateau de l'Oesling — *Eislek* en Luxembourgeois — connaît un climat particulier, plus froid et humide qu'ailleurs. En hiver, les chutes de neige y sont parfois si abondantes que l'on plante de hauts piquets rouges et blancs sur les bords des petites routes. Jusqu'au milieu du XIXe siècle, les villageois de l'Oesling vivaient dans l'isolement, quasi sans lien avec le reste du pays. Aujourd'hui, il en est tout autrement : au printemps, les foules se pressent pour assister aux courses nautiques nationales et internationales, qui se déroulent sur la Wiltz et la Clerve.

The river Wiltz, after coiling gracefully through a valley edged by narrow fields and encircled by wooded hills, flows into the Clerve at **Kautenbach**, a little village of about 200 souls. The plateau of the Oesling — *Eislek* in the Luxembourg language — has a very special climate, colder and more humid than elsewhere. In winter the snowfall is often so heavy that tall red and white stakes are planted along the edges of the small roads. Until the middle of the 19th century the villagers of the Oesling lived in isolation, nearly without contact with the rest of the country. It is quite different today: in spring crowds arrive to watch the national and international boat races on the Wiltz and the Clerve.

Nachdem sich die Wiltz elegant durch ein von engen Wiesen umrandetes und von bewaldeten Hügeln umgebenes Tal geschlängelt hat, fließt sie in **Kautenbach**, einem Dorf mit rund 200 Einwohnern, in die Clerf. Das Plateau von Ösling — auf Luxemburgisch *Eislek* — ist durch ein besonderes Klima geprägt, das kälter und feuchter ist als anderswo. Im Winter sind die Schneefälle dort zuweilen so erheblich, dass an die Ränder der kleinen Straßen rote und weiße Pflöcke gesetzt werden. Bis zur Mitte des 19. Jhs. lebten die Dorfbewohner des Ösling isoliert, nahezu ohne eine Verbindung zum übrigen Land. Heute ist dies völlig anders: Im Frühjahr drängen sich die Menschenmengen, um die nationalen und internationalen Wasserrennen auf Wiltz und Clerf anzusehen.

Na zijn sierlijke tocht door een vallei die met smalle weiden en beboste heuvels is afgeboord, mondt de Wiltz uit in de Clerve in **Kautenbach**, een dorp met zowat 200 inwoners. Het plateau van de Oesling — *Eislek* in het Luxemburgs — heeft een heel apart klimaat, het is er kouder en vochtiger dan elders. In de winter is de sneeuwval soms zo fel dat er hoge rode en witte staken langs de kleine weggetjes worden uitgezet. Tot in het midden van de 19de eeuw woonden de dorpelingen van de Oesling afgezonderd, bijna zonder enige verbinding met de rest van het land. Dat is vandaag wel heel anders: in de lente stroomt de massa toe om niets te missen van de nationale en internationale waterwedstrijden op de Wiltz en de Clerve.

Près du frontispice courbe de l'hôtel de ville de Wiltz, face à l'entrée du château, la croix de justice sculptée en 1502 rappelle les droits de franchise et de marché accordés à la ville par le comte Godart de Wiltz. Y sont adossées les statues de la Vierge et de saint Jean Népomucène.

Abondant en espaces réservés aux camps, **Wiltz** est surnommée la «capitale européenne du scoutisme».

In der Nähe des gebogenen Rathaus-Frontispiz gegenüber dem Schlosseingang erinnert das 1502 geschnitzte Justizkreuz an die Freiheits- und Marktrechte, die der Stadt vom Grafen Godart von Wiltz gewährt worden sind. Daran lehnen die Statuen der Heiligen Jungfrau und des Heiligen Johannes Nepomuk.

Da es viele Zeltlager-Flächen gibt, trägt **Wiltz** den Beinamen „europäische Hauptstadt der Pfadfinder".

Standing near the curved frontispiece of the Town Hall and facing the entrance to the chateau is the Cross of Justice, carved in 1502, signifying the right to vote and to hold a market accorded to the town by Count Godart of Wiltz. Statues of the Virgin and of Saint John Nepomuk lean against it.

Wiltz has reserved many areas for camping and is called "the European capital of the Scout movement".

Vlakbij de voorgevel van het stadhuis, tegenover de ingang van kasteel, herinnert het gesculpteerde gerechtskruis uit 1502 aan de vrijheids- en markt-rechten die graaf Godart van Wiltz aan de stad ver-leende. De beelden die er tegenaan leunen, zijn van de Maagd Maria en Sint-Jan-Nepomucenus.

Wiltz beschikt over zeer uitgestrekte ideale ruimtes voor kampen en kreeg daarom de bijnaam "scouting-hoofdstad van Europa".

Admirablement située sur un versant de l'Oesling, **Wiltz** se répartit en une partie basse où pointe la tour romane de l'église gothique et une partie haute couronnée par le château conquis par les Bourguignons et reconstruit durant les XVIIe et XVIIIe siècles. Vendu aux enchères par les révolutionnaires français, endommagé lors de l'offensive von Rundstedt, il appartient depuis 1951 à l'État luxembourgeois qui a transformé le corps de logis en maison de retraite et les dépendances en musée.

Das herrlich auf einem Ösling-Hang gelegene **Wiltz** besteht aus einem unteren Teil, in dem sich der romanische Turm der gotischen Kirche erhebt, und einem oberen Teil, der von dem durch die Burgunder eroberten und im 17. und 18. Jh. wieder aufgebauten Schloss gekrönt wird. Das Schloss, das von den französischen Revolutionären versteigert und bei der Offensive von Rundstedts beschädigt wurde, gehört seit 1951 dem luxemburgischen Staat, der den Hauptbau zu einem Altersheim und die Nebengebäude zu einem Museum umgebaut hat.

Wiltz, well situated on a slope of the Oesling, is divided into a lower town where the Romanesque tower of the Gothic church rises and an upper part dominated by a castle conquered by the Burgundians and rebuilt during the 17th and 18th centuries. The castle was auctioned off by the French revolutionaries and heavily damaged during the von Rundstedt offensive. Since 1951 it has belonged to the Luxembourg State which has transformed the main part into a retirement home and the outbuildings into a museum.

Op een helling van de Oesling koestert **Wiltz** zich. De prachtig gelegen gemeente bestaat uit een laag gedeelte waar de romaanse toren van de gotische kerk uitsteekt, en een hoog gedeelte dat bekroond wordt door het kasteel dat de Bourgondiërs veroverden en dat in de 17de en de 18de eeuw werd heropgebouwd. Het werd per opbod verkocht door de Franse revolutionairen, beschadigd tijdens het von Rundstedt offensief en is sinds 1951 eigendom van de staat Luxemburg die het woongedeelte ombouwde tot rusthuis en de bijgebouwen tot museum.

◄◄▲

Tumultueuse par endroits, **la Clerve** s'insinue dans des vallées étroites et tortueuses. Encastrée dans l'une d'elle, entourée de collines boisées, **Clervaux** est bâtie autour d'un promontoire où Gérard de Spontheim, frère du comte de Vianden, implanta un château au XIIᵉ siècle. La forteresse primitive fut considérablement agrandie au cours du XVᵉ siècle. Aux XVIIᵉ et XVIIIᵉ siècles, elle s'étendit en château de plaisance. Celui-ci était en mauvais état lorsque, en décembre 1944, les troupes américaines s'y défendirent contre les assauts des Allemands. Ils ne purent maîtriser l'incendie qui le ravagea. Après la guerre, il fut largement reconstruit par le gouvernement luxembourgeois à partir des plans anciens.

The **Clerve**, turbulent in some areas, winds through narrow, twisting valleys. **Clervaux**, nestled in one of them and surrounded by wooded hills, is built around a promontory where Gerard of Spontheim, brother of the Count of Vianden, erected a castle in the 12th century. The original fortress was greatly enlarged during the 15th century. In the 17th and 18th centuries it was used as a country retreat. It was in poor condition when American troops had to defend it from German attack. They could not extinguish the fire that raged through it. After the war the Luxembourg government following the old plans rebuilt most of it.

Die stellenweise unruhige **Clerf** zieht sich durch enge und gewundene Täler. Das in einem dieser Täler eingeschlossene, von bewaldeten Hügeln umgebene **Clervaux** ist um eine Landspitze herum gebaut, auf der der Bruder des Grafen von Vianden, Gerhard von Spontheim, im 12. Jh. ein Schloss errichtete. Im 15. Jh. wurde die ursprüngliche Festung erheblich vergrößert und im 17. und 18. Jh. zu einem Lustschloss erweitert. Dieses war in schlechtem Zustand, als die amerikanischen Truppen sich dort im Dezember 1944 gegen die Angriffe der Deutschen verteidigten. Sie konnten den Brand, der es verwüstete, nicht unter Kontrolle bringen. Nach dem Krieg wurde es von der luxemburgischen Regierung nach alten Plänen weitgehend wieder aufgebaut.

De hier en daar toch wel onstuimige **Clerve** kronkelt zich door nauwe en bochtige valleien. In één van die bochten ligt **Clervaux** genesteld, helemaal omgeven door beboste hellingen. De stad is gebouwd rond een kaap die Gerard van Spontheim, broer van de graaf van Vianden, in de 12de eeuw uitkoos voor zijn kasteel. De primitieve vesting werd aanzienlijk vergroot in de loop van de 15de eeuw. In de 17de en de 18de eeuw werd het een lustslot. Dit was al in slechte staat toen de Amerikaanse strijdkrachten er zich in december 1944 verschansten om de aanvallen van de Duitsers af te slaan. Ze konden niet beletten dat een brand het hele kasteel verwoestte. Na de oorlog besloot de Luxemburgse regering het grotendeels terug op te bouwen, op basis van de oude plannen.

Pages 120 à 124

Modeste village niché dans un décor de prairies et de bois, près d'Houffalize en Belgique, **Hachiville** doit sa réputation à son église paroissiale. Son intérieur s'apparente à un petit musée de l'art religieux populaire d'autrefois. Pour réaliser le mobilier naïvement décoré, les artisans se sont complus dans les fantaisies du style rococo. Mais un chef d'œuvre s'impose au regard : le retable gothico-Renaissance, qui raconte des épisodes de la vie de la Vierge et des scènes de la Passion du Christ. Le réalisme et la polychromie des groupes sculptés, le bleu de certains vêtements, la carnation pâle pour les femmes, plus soutenue pour les hommes, la séparation des compartiments par des colonnettes, tout indique la provenance d'un atelier brabançon du milieu du XVIᵉ siècle.

Seite 120 bis 124

Hachiville, ein kleines Dorf, das in der Nähe von Houffalize in Belgien inmitten von Wiesen und Wäldern liegt, verdankt seinen Ruf seiner Pfarrkirche. Ihr Inneres gleicht einem kleinen Museum der religiösen Volkskunst von früher. Für das naiv verzierte Mobiliar haben die Künstler die Originalität des Rokoko-Stils genutzt. Aber ein Meisterwerk zieht den Blick auf sich: der Gotik-Renaissance-Altaraufsatz, der Ereignisse aus dem Leben der Jungfrau Maria und Szenen aus der Passion Christi erzählt. Die realistische Darstellung und die Mehrfarbigkeit der Gruppen, das Blau einiger Kleidungsstücke, die bleiche Hautfarbe der Frauen, die etwas dunklere der Männer, und die Trennung der Abteilungen durch kleine Säulen: Alles weist auf die Herkunft aus einem Brabanter Atelier Mitte des 16. Jhs. hin.

Pages 120 to 124

Hachiville, a small village nestled in a landscape of fields and woods, near Houffalize in Belgium, owes its fame to its parish church. Its interior resembles a small museum of the popular religious art of bygone days. The spirit of the rococo style inspired the artisans who made the naively decorated furniture, the statues and the altars in the side aisles. There is, however, a masterpiece to be seen: the carved Gothic-Renaissance retable recounting episodes in the life of the Virgin and scenes of the Passion of Christ. The realism and the polychrome of the carved groups, the blue of certain garments, the pale complexions of the women and the darker skin of the men, the separation of the compartments by small columns, all indicate that it was made in a Brabant workshop in the mid 16th century.

Pagina 120 tot 124

Vlakbij het Belgische Houffalize ligt een bescheiden dorp, in een vredig landschap van weiden en bossen. Het is **Hachiville** dat zijn faam dankt aan zijn parochiekerk. Het interieur heeft veel weg van een klein museum van de eertijdse religieuze volkskunst. Voor de versiering van het meubilair in naïeve stijl en van de beelden en zijaltaren zochten de ambachtslieden hun inspiratie in de fantasie van de rococo. Maar een meesterwerk eist de aandacht op: het retabel van houtsnijwerk in renaissance-gotiek, dat gebeurtenissen uit het leven van de Maagd Maria vertelt en taferelen uit de Christus-passie voorstelt. Het realisme en de polychromie van de figuren, het blauw van bepaalde kledingstukken, de bleke huidskleur van de vrouwen, die iets meer uitgesproken is voor de mannen, de scheiding van de vakken door zuiltjes, wijzen er allemaal op dat hier een Brabants atelier uit het midden van de 16de eeuw aan het werk was.

C'est à la petite chapelle de l'er-
mitage Saint-Thomas ou **Helzerklaus** à **Hachiville** que l'on doit
l'étonnante présence du grand
polyptyque dans ce village. Il y
était jadis conservé mais — les
voleurs d'objets d'art sévissaient
dès les années cinquante — il fut
transféré dans la proche église
paroissiale.

Der kleinen Kapelle der
Einsiedelei St. Thomas oder
Helzerklaus in **Hachiville** ist das
überraschende Vorhandensein der
großen Polyptyque in diesem Dorf
zu verdanken. Früher wurde sie in
der Kapelle aufbewahrt, aber da
Kunstdiebe in den 50er Jahren dort
ihr Unwesen trieben, wurde sie in
die nahe gelegene Pfarrkirche
umgesiedelt.

The little chapel of Saint
Thomas's hermitage or **Helzerklaus** in **Hachiville** once housed
the large and astonishing polyp-
tych of the village. It was moved to
the parish church in the 1950's
because of the prevalence of thefts
of art.

Het is aan de kleine kapel van de
hermitage Sint Thomas of **Helzerklaus** in **Hachiville** te danken dat
men in dit dorp verrassend de grote
polyptiek aantreft. Vroeger werd
deze in de kapel bewaard, maar na
de teistering door kunstdieven in de
jaren 50 actief werd de polyptiek
overgebracht naar de parochiekerk
in de buurt.

Les eaux de la Troine ont été détournées pour être captées par les aubes des roues du moulin d'**Asselborn**. À l'intérieur du bâtiment est entreposé le matériel servant à transporter les grains et à en séparer les graviers et autres impuretés. Au sortir des meules _(en haut)_, le mélange de farine, de gruau et de son devait être bluté dans des plansichters _(en bas)_. L'appareillage du moulin est en parfait état de marche. Il fonctionne... au cours de la saison touristique.

Das Wasser der Troine ist zu den Schaufeln der Räder der Mühle von **Asselborn** umgeleitet worden. Im Innern des Gebäudes ist das Material gelagert, das zum Transport des Korns und der Abscheidung von Kieseln und anderen Unreinheiten diente. Nach Passieren der Mühlsteine _(oben)_ sollte die Mischung aus Mehl und Kleie in _Plansichtern_ _(unten)_ gesiebt werden. Das Gerät der Mühle ist in betriebsbereitem Zustand und funktioniert... in der Touristensaison.

The waters of the Troine have been diverted to serve the paddlewheel of the mill of **Asselborn**. Material used to transport the grain and to separate it from stones and other impurities are deposited in the interior of the building. After coming out from the millstones _(above)_ the mixture of flour, groats and bran had to be sifted in the _plansichters_ _(below)_. The mechanism of the mill is in perfect working order and functions... during the tourist season.

De waters van de Troine werden afgeleid om het schoepenrad van de molen van **Asselborn** aan de gang te houden. In het gebouw is het materiaal opgeslagen dat dient om het graan te vervoeren en om de kiezel en andere onzuiverheden te verwijderen. Na de behandeling door de molenstenen _(boven)_ moest het mengsel van bloem, grutten en zemelen gezift in _plansichters_ _(onder)_. De apparatuur van de molen is nog altijd in perfecte staat en werkt... tijdens het toeristisch seizoen.

À la limite de l'Oesling et du Gutland, **Diekirch** n'enorgueillit d'un passé romain qu'attestent de nombreux vestiges — hypocaustes, mosaïques visibles au musée local qui expose aussi de nombreux objets de la vie quotidienne — dégagés lors des fouilles. L'église Saint-Laurent (1467) occupe l'emplacement d'un sanctuaire romain dont des traces de mur sont visible dans la paroi méridionale. Quant à l'église paroissiale de style néo-roman, ses deux tours parallèles se voient de loin.

Faut-il le préciser ? La ville doit sa renommée à la brasserie qui produit la bière savoureuse qui porte son nom.

Das an der Grenze zwischen Ösling und Gutland gelegene **Diekirch** ist stolz auf sein romanisches Erbe, von dem zahlreiche, bei Ausgrabungen frei gelegte Überreste zeugen: Hypocausten und Mosaiken, die im Ortsmuseum, das auch zahlreiche Gegenstände des täglichen Lebens zeigt, zu sehen sind. Die Sankt Laurentiuskirche (1467) steht an der Stelle eines romanischen Heiligtums, von dem in der Südwand Mauerspuren sichtbar sind. Die beiden parallelen Türme der neuromanischen Pfarrkirche sind weithin sichtbar.

Muss eigens darauf hingewiesen werden? Die Stadt verdankt ihre Bekanntheit der Brauerei, die das nach ihr benannte wohlschmeckende Bier braut.

Diekirch, lying on the edge of the Oesling and the Gutland, is proud not only of its Roman past that can be seen in numerous vestiges such as the hypocausts and the mosaics that are housed in the local museum along with a multitude of everyday objects found in the archaeological digs. There is also the church of Saint Laurence (1467), built on the site of a Roman sanctuary, traces of which can be seen in the south wall. The two parallel towers of the neo-Romanesque parish church can be seen from far away.

Must one really state it? The town owes its fame to the brewery producing the excellent beer that carries its name.

Aan de grens van de Oesling en van het Gutland, kan **Diekirch** bogen op een boeiend Romeins verleden, zoals blijkt uit de talrijke overblijfselen — hypocausta en mozaïeken die te bezichtigen zijn in het plaatselijk museum, naast tal van voorwerpen uit het dagelijks leven die bij de opgravingen aan de oppervlakte kwamen. Op de plaats waar nu de kerk Saint-Laurent (1467) staat, lag vroeger een Romeins sanctuarium. In de zuidelijke wand zijn trouwens nog sporen van de muur uit die tijd te zien. De parochiekerk in neo-romaanse stijl is van ver te herkennen aan zijn twee evenwijdige torens.

En moet het nog gezegd? De stad is vooral vermaard om het lekkere bier dat haar naam draagt.

Ci-dessus et pages 130 à 133

Vers la fin du mois de mai, les genêts recouvrent d'un manteau doré le moutonnement des buttes qui entourent Lipperscheid, non loin du site fortifié de Bourscheid.

Sur le sommet rocheux de Buerbierg, le château fort de **Bourscheid** assurait, dès le XIᵉ siècle, le contrôle des vallées de la Sûre, qui coule en contrebas, de la Wark et de la Blees. Il fut considérablement agrandi au cours des XIVᵉ et XVᵉ siècles. Le dernier descendant de la famille de Bourscheid mourut en 1512, ce qui marqua le début de la décadence de la forteresse. L'État luxembourgeois a entrepris de le relever de ses ruines avec l'aide d'une association locale.

Above and pages 130 to 133

Towards the end of May, broom covers with a golden mantle the numerous hillocks that surround Lipperscheid, not far from the fortified site of Bourscheid.

The fortress of **Bourscheid**, built on the rocky summit of the Buerbierg ensured as early as the 11th century control of the valleys of the Sûre that flows below, of the Wark and the Blees. It was greatly enlarged during the 14th and 15th centuries. The last descendant of the Bourscheid family dies in 1512, marking the decline and ruin of the fortress. The State of Luxembourg has begun restoration work with the help of a local association.

Oben und Seite 130 bis 133

Ende Mai überzieht der Ginster die wogenden Hügel, die das nicht weit von der Festung von Bourscheid gelegene Lipperscheid umgeben, mit einem goldenen Mantel.

Auf der felsigen Höhe von Buerbierg gewährleistete die Burg von **Bourscheid** ab dem 11. Jh. die Kontrolle über die Täler der weiter unten verlaufenden Sauer sowie der Wark und der Blees. Im 14. und 15. Jh. wurde sie erheblich erweitert. Der letzte Nachkomme der Familie Bourscheid verstarb 1512. Dies war der Beginn des Niedergangs der Festung. Der luxemburgische Staat hat es sich zur Aufgabe gemacht, mit Hilfe einer lokalen Vereinigung ihren Wiederaufbau zu betreiben.

Hierboven en pagina 130 tot 133

Tegen eind mei legt de brem een gulden mantel over het kroes van de heuveltjes rond Lipperscheid, niet ver van het versterkte Bourscheid.

Hoog op de rotspiek van de Buerbierg hield de vesting van **Bourscheid**, vanaf de 11de eeuw, toezicht op de valleien van de lager gelegen Sûre, de Wark en de Blees. Ze werd fors groter gemaakt in de 14de en in de 15de eeuw. De laatste afstammeling van de familie van Bourscheid stierf in 1512, waarna het fort aan zijn lot werd overgelaten. De Luxemburgse staat bundelde ondertussen de krachten met een lokale vereniging om het kasteel weer op te trekken.

Depuis le traité des XXIV Articles qui, mis en application en 1839, a établi l'indépendance du grand-duché, **l'Our** marque la majeure partie de la frontière naturelle du Luxembourg avec l'Allemagne. Le village de Bivels a été bâti au centre d'une gigantesque boucle de la rivière. Non loin de là, un barrage de 26 mètres de hauteur a créé un lac de retenue qui s'étend sur environ 8 kilomètres. L'eau du lac est pompée vers deux bassins en haut du mont Saint-Nicolas puis déversée dans les cavernes où est installée la centrale hydroélectrique qui fournit 1,6 millions de kilowatts-heure par an.

Since the Treaty of the XXIV Articles, establishing the independence of Luxembourg in 1839, was applied **the Our** has delimited the greater part of the natural frontier between Luxembourg and Germany. The village of Bivels has been built in the centre of a huge bend in the river. Not far from there a 26-meter high dam has created a reservoir extending over nearly 8 kilometres. The lake water is pumped up to two ponds on top of Saint Nicholas mount and then poured into the caves where a hydroelectric station provides 1.6 million-kilowatt hours a year.

Seit dem 1839 in Kraft getretenen 24-Artikel-Vertrag, der die Unabhängigkeit Luxemburgs begründete, bildet **die Our** den größten Teil der natürlichen Grenze zwischen Luxemburg und Deutschland. Das Dorf Bivels wurde in der Mitte einer enormen Schleife des Flusses errichtet. Nicht weit davon entfernt hat ein 26 Meter hoher Staudamm einen rund acht Kilometer langen Stausee geschaffen. Das Wasser des Sees wird in zwei Becken oben auf dem Nikolausberg gepumpt und gelangt anschließend in die Kavernen, wo sich das Pumpspeicherkraftwerk befindet, das 1,6 Millionen Kilowattstunden pro Jahr erzeugt.

Sinds het verdrag van de Vierentwintig Artikelen, dat in 1839 in voege kwam, Luxemburg onafhankelijk maakte, wordt het grootste deel van de natuurlijke grens tussen Luxemburg en Duitsland gevormd door **de Our**. Het dorp Bivels werd gebouwd midden in een reuzegrote lus van de rivier. Een steenworp verder werd met een dam van 26 meter hoog een stuwmeer van ongeveer 8 kilometer aangelegd. Het water van het meer wordt naar twee spaarbekkens boven op de Mont Saint-Nicolas gepompt en daarna in een ondergrondse waterkrachtcentrale gestort die 1,6 miljoen kilowatt/uur per jaar levert.

Bien sûr, **Vianden** c'est d'abord le château fort dont la construction débuta au IXe siècle et qui connut ses principaux agrandissements aux XIIe et XIIIe siècles. Plusieurs dynasties se le disputèrent : les puissants seigneurs locaux puis les comtes de Luxembourg et ensuite les Nassau. Laissé à l'abandon au XIXe siècle, servant de carrière — Victor Hugo qui séjourna à Vianden le décrit comme une ruine sinistre — le château devint en 1977 la propriété de l'État qui réalisa sa restauration dans son état originel. Romanes ou gothiques, ses salles des chevaliers, des comtes, d'armes, sa chapelle, sa cuisine permettent à nouveau d'imaginer la vie intense de jadis.

Deux pages suivantes
Mais Vianden c'est aussi la vieille ville protégée par une enceinte fortifiée, son hôtel de ville — ancienne maison féodale de 1469 où logeait un assesseur du tribunal —, son église gothique bâtie en 1248 comme église abbatiale du monastère des Trinitaires.

Vianden ist natürlich zunächst die Burg aus dem 9. Jh., die hauptsächlich im 12. und 13. Jh. erweitert wurde. Mehrere Dynastien machten sich die Burg streitig: die mächtigen lokalen Herren, dann die Grafen von Luxemburg und schließlich die Nassauer. Die im 19. Jh. sich selbst überlassene und als Steinbruch dienende Burg — Victor Hugo, der sich in Vianden aufhielt, beschrieb sie als düstere Ruine — wurde 1977 Eigentum des Staates, der ihre Restauration in ihren ursprünglichen Zustand vornahm. Die romanischen bzw. gotischen Ritter-, Grafen- und Waffensäle sowie ihre Kapelle und die Küche versetzen den Besucher wieder in die Lage, sich das rege Leben von einst vorzustellen.

Zwei folgende Seiten
Aber Vianden ist auch die von einer Befestigungsmauer geschützte Altstadt, das Rathaus, ein ehemaliges Feudalhaus von 1469, in dem ein Gerichtsbeisitzer wohnte und die 1248 als Abteikirche des Dreifaltigkeitsklosters errichtete gotische Kirche.

Vianden is first of all the castle, construction of which began in the 9th century with major additions in the 12th and 13th centuries. Several dynasties competed for it: the powerful local lords and then the Counts of Luxembourg and later the House of Nassau. Abandoned in the 19th century, it was used as a quarry — Victor Hugo who stayed at Vianden described it as a sinister ruin. The castle became State property in 1977 and was restored to its original state. The halls of the knights and of the Counts, the armoury, the chapel and the kitchen, some Romanesque and some Gothic, help us to imagine the intense activity of the past.

Following two pages
But Vianden is also the old town, protected by fortifications, its Town Hall, the old feudal house of 1469 where the court assistant lived, and its Gothic church built in 1248 to serve as the abbey church of the Trinitarian monastery.

Uiteraard is **Vianden** eerst en vooral de burcht waarvan de eerste steen werd gelegd in de 9de eeuw en die daarna nog enkele uitbreidingen onderging, onder meer in de 12de en in de 13de eeuw. Deze werd een twistappel tussen verschillende dynastieën: de machtige lokale heren en daarna de graven van Luxemburg en vervolgens de Nassau's. Maar in de 19de eeuw bekommerde niemand er zich nog om en werd het een steengroeve. Victor Hugo, die in Vianden verbleef, beschreef het als een onheilspellende ruïne. In 1977 werd de vesting echter eigendom van de staat, die ze in haar oorspronkelijke staat herstelde. De ridder- en gravenzalen, de wapenzalen en de kapel, de keuken schetsen een waarheidsgetrouw beeld van het drukke leven van toen.

Volgende twee pagina's
Maar Vianden is ook de oude stad die wordt beschermd door een versterkte wal, een fraai stadhuis — een vroeger feodaal huis uit 1469 waar een bijstaand rechter verbleef — en een gotische kerk die in 1248 werd gebouwd als abdijkerk van het klooster van de Trinitariërs.

Le tissu urbain médiéval a survécu à **Vianden**. Dans la grand-rue, les maisons de maître des XVIIᵉ et XVIIIᵉ siècles demeurées intactes rivalisent de charme et d'un certain faste bourgeois, que révèle souvent le décor sculpté qui encadre les entrées aux belles portes de chêne. Dominant le bourg en contrebas du château, sur la saillie d'un rocher, la tour de guet carrée faisait partie de l'enceinte fortifiée qui entourait la ville.

Das mittelalterliche Stadtbild hat sich in **Vianden** gehalten. Die in der Grand-Rue stehenden Herrenhäuser aus dem 17. und 18. Jh. übertreffen einander in Charme und einem gewissen bürgerlichen Prunk, der häufig in dem verzierten Schmuck, der die mit schönen Eichentüren versehenen Eingänge umrahmt, zum Ausdruck kommt. Der eckige Wachturm, der den Marktflecken unterhalb des Schlosses auf einem Felsvorsprung beherrscht, war Teil der Befestigungsanlage, die die Stadt umgab.

The mediaeval urban infrastructure has survived in **Vianden**. Charming mansions of the 17th and 18th centuries in their original state line the Grand-Rue demonstrating, by the carved ornamentation framing their handsome oak doors, a period of comfortable prosperity. Below the castle a square watchtower on a ledge of rock, once part of the fortified wall around the city, dominates the landscape.

Het middeleeuws stedelijk weefsel bleef onaangeroerd in **Vianden**. In de hoofdstraat wedijveren de nog mooi bewaarde herenhuizen uit de 17de en de 18de eeuw met elkaar in charme. Er straalt een zekere burgerlijke praal van uit, vooral dan van het gesculpteerde decor rond de mooie houten ingangspoorten. De vierkante uitkijktoren die op een rotsuitsteeksel uittorent boven het dorp aan de voet van het kasteel, maakte deel uit van de versterkte omwalling rond de stad.

En 1216, les Trinitaires avaient été appelés de Picardie par le comte Philippe et la comtesse de Vianden. Leur monastère dont les bâtiments se développèrent jusqu'au XVIIIe siècle fut supprimé par l'empereur Joseph II en 1783.

Derrière le couvent devenu maison de retraite, on a réussi à restaurer le **cloître** des Trinitaires, partiellement détruit au cours de la Deuxième Guerre mondiale. D'un style gothique très dépouillé, il présente de sobres ogives trilobées et abrite plusieurs pierres tombales dont celle de Henri de Nassau mort en 1589.

Im Jahre 1216 war der Dreifaltigkeitsorden von Graf Philipp und der Gräfin von Vianden aus der Picardie gerufen worden. Sein Kloster, dessen Gebäude bis zum 18. Jh. erweitert wurden, wurde von Kaiser Joseph II. im Jahre 1783 geschlossen.

Hinter dem zu einem Altersheim umgebauten Kloster konnte der im Zweiten Weltkrieg teilweise zerstörte **Kreuzgang** des Dreifaltigkeitsordens wieder aufgebaut werden. Der in einem sehr nüchternen gotischen Stil gehaltene Kreuzgang zeigt schmucklose Kleeblattbögen und beherbergt mehrere Grabsteine, darunter den des 1589 verstorbenen Heinrich von Nassau.

In 1216 Count Philip and his Countess summoned the Trinitarians of Picardy to Vianden. The monastery, construction of which continued into the 18th century, was suppressed by Emperor Joseph II in 1783.

Behind the monastery, now a retirement home, a **cloister** partly destroyed during World War II has been restored. Built in an austere Gothic style it has trefoil ogives and contains several gravestones, one of which is that of Henry of Nassau who died in 1589.

In 1216 haalden graaf Filips en de gravin van Vianden de Trinitariërs van Picardië naar deze contreien. De kloostergebouwen kenden een gestage ontwikkeling tot in de 18de eeuw, toen keizer Jozef II het klooster afschafte in 1783.

De **kruisgang** achter het klooster, nu een rusthuis, werd in de tweede wereldoorlog deels verwoest maar is nu mooi gerestaureerd. Hij is opgetrokken in een zeer sobere gotische stijl, met eenvoudige drielobbige spitsbogen en huisvest enkele grafstenen, zoals van Hendrik van Nassau die in 1589 overleed.

Ernz blanche et Ernz noire

Weiße Ernz und schwarze Ernz

Depuis leurs sources au cœur du Grünewald, la forêt aux portes de la capitale, l'Ernz blanche et l'Ernz noire sinuent parmi les collines du centre du Gutland. Elles ne tardent pas à pénétrer dans une région au relief abrupt qui reçut au XIXᵉ siècle le surnom de «petite Suisse», où elles grossiront d'innombrables ruisseaux et 'baach' avant de se jeter dans la Sûre. Ci-dessus : l'Ernz noire en amont de Grondhaff.

Von ihrer Quelle mitten im vor der Hauptstadt gelegenen Grünewald schlängeln sich die weiße und die schwarze Ernz zwischen den Hügeln des mittleren Gutlands hindurch. Bald darauf treten sie in eine Region mit steilem Relief ein, das im 19. Jh. den Beinamen „kleine Schweiz" erhielt. Dort nehmen sie unzählige Bäche und ‚Baach' auf, um schließlich in die Sauer zu fließen. Oben: die schwarze Ernz vor Grondhaff.

The White Ernz and the Black Ernz
De witte Ernz en de zwarte Ernz

The White Ernz and the Black Ernz rise in the heart of the Grünewald, the forest close to the capital and wind through the hills in the centre of the Gutland. They soon arrive in a region of abrupt strata that was nicknamed "little Switzerland" in the 19th century. They are swollen by numerous streams and 'baachs' before joining the Sûre. Above: the Black Ernz upstream from Grondhaaf.

Van hun bron in het hart van het Grünewald, het woud aan de poorten van de hoofdstad, trekken de witte Ernz en de zwarte Ernz door de heuvels van het centrum van het Gutland. Ze komen al snel terecht in een streek met een steil reliëf die in de 19de eeuw de bijnaam "Klein-Zwitserland" kreeg, en waar ze aandikken met tal van beekjes en 'baach' om zich dan in de Sûre te storten. Hierboven: de zwarte Ernz stroomopwaarts van Grondhaff.

Au pays des influents seigneurs de Linster, le robuste donjon du château fort de **Bourglinster** date du début du XIᵉ siècle. Il fut complété au XIVᵉ de l'entrée principale, son pont d'accès et ses deux tours. Des éléments des styles baroque et Renaissance s'ajoutèrent par la suite. Au XVIIIᵉ siècle, le château appartenait à deux familles, les von Waldeck et les d'Orley; seule la chapelle castrale leur était commune. Restauré par l'État qui l'acquit en 1968, il est régulièrement le cadre de manifestations culturelles.

Der im Lande der einflussreichen Herren von Linster gelegene stämmige Bergfried der Burg von **Bourglinster** stammt aus dem Beginn des 11. Jhs. Im 14. Jh. kamen der Haupteingang, die Zugangsbrücke und die beiden Türme hinzu. Es folgten Barock- und Renaissanceelemente. Im 18. Jh. gehörte die Burg den beiden Familien von Waldeck und Orley. Nur die Burgkapelle war gemeinsamer Besitz. In der 1968 vom Staat gekauften und restaurierten Burg finden regelmäßig kulturelle Veranstaltungen statt.

The robust keep of the fortress of **Bourglinster**, in the country of the powerful lords of Linster, dates from the early 11th century. It was completed in the 14th century by the addition of the main gate, the drawbridge and two towers. Baroque and Renaissance elements were added later. In the 18th century the castle belonged to two families called von Waldeck and d'Orley. The only space they shared was the castle chapel. Restored by the State after its acquisition in 1968, it is now used regularly for cultural events.

In het land van de invloedrijke heren van Linster, dateert de robuuste donjon van de vesting van **Bourglinster** uit het begin van de 11de eeuw. Hij werd in de 14de eeuw aangevuld met de hoofdingang, zijn brug en zijn twee torens. Daarna kwamen er nog elementen uit de barok en de renaissance bij. In de 18de eeuw behoorde het kasteel toe aan twee families, von Waldeck en d'Orley; enkel de kasteelkapel was gemeenschappelijk. In 1968 kocht de staat het over en nu vinden er regelmatig culturele manifestaties plaats.

Au village, qui repose sur un plateau de grès dominant la vallée de l'Ernz blanche, les habitants ont participé à la restauration des maisons dont les façades ont reçu des teintes proches de celles des sables du Gutland; le civisme n'est pas un vain mot au Luxembourg. Une maison de maître du XVIIIᵉ siècle coiffée d'une haute toiture à la Mansard a été transformée en auberge de jeunesse.

Die Einwohner des Dorfes, das auf einem Kalkplateau, das das Tal der weißen Ernz beherrscht, ruht, haben sich an der Restaurierung der Häuser, deren Fassaden in den Färbungen des Gutlands-Sands gestrichen wurden, beteiligt. Bürgersinn ist in Luxemburg kein leeres Wort. Ein mit einem hohen Mansardendach gedecktes Herrenhaus aus dem 18. Jh. wurde in eine Jugendherberge umgewandelt.

In the village, lying on a sandstone plateau overlooking the White Ernz, the citizens have leagued together to restore the houses, the façades of which are painted in shades much like that of the Gutland sands: public spiritedness is widely practiced in Luxembourg. An 18th century mansion with a high mansard roof now serves as a youth hostel.

In het dorp, dat rust op een plateau van zandsteen dat de vallei van de witte Ernz domineert, werkten de bewoners mee aan de restauratie van de huizen. De gevels kregen de tint van het zand van het Gutland; in Luxemburg is burgerzin geen ijdel woord. Een herenhuis uit de 18de eeuw, met een hoog mansardedak, werd omgebouwd tot jeugdherberg.

En bordure du Müllerthal, à l'emplacement d'un ancien rempart carolingien, les von der Felz, seigneurs de **Larochette** et comme tels vassaux du comte de Luxembourg, construisirent le château qui prit toute son ampleur au XIVᵉ siècle sous les Hombourg et les Créhange. Incendié en 1567 puis laissé à l'abandon, il ne fut restauré qu'à partir des années 1980. La *Homburger Haus* du début du XVᵉ siècle borde un piton rocheux; Jules Verne y séjourna pendant quelques semaines.

Le village s'ordonne dans la combe formée par la courbe de l'Ernz blanche; au clocher de l'église paroissiale, la cloche qui appelle les fidèles provient du château.

La majorité des habitants de Larochette sont d'origine portugaise; conséquence de l'immigration la plus importante d'Europe, la population du Luxembourg est composée de plus de trente pour cent d'étrangers.

Am Rande des Müllerthals haben die von der Felz — Herren von **Larochette** und als solche Vasallen des Grafen von Luxemburg — an der Stelle einer ehemaligen karolingischen Befestigungsmauer das Schloss erbaut, das im 14. Jh. unter Homburgern und Criechingern seine volle Größe erreichte. Das 1567 ausgebrannte und dann sich selbst überlassene Schloss wurde erst ab den 1980er Jahren restauriert. Das *Homburger Haus* von Anfang des 15. Jhs. säumt eine Bergspitze. Jules Verne hat sich dort einige Wochen lang aufgehalten.

Das Dorf liegt in dem von der Biegung der weißen Ernz gebildeten Erosionstal. Die Glocke im Glockenturm der Pfarrkirche, die die Gläubigen ruft, stammt aus dem Schloss.

Die Mehrheit der Einwohner von Larochette sind portugiesischer Herkunft. Infolge der stärksten Immigration Europas besteht die luxemburgische Bevölkerung zu mehr als 30 Prozent aus Ausländern.

The von der Felz, lords of **Larochette** and thus vassals of the Count of Luxembourg, built a castle on the site of an old Carolingian rampart on the edge of the Müllerthal. The castle was enlarged in the 14th century by the Hombourg and the Crehange families who later owned it. It burned down in 1567 and abandoned. It was only restored in the 1980's. The *Homburger House* built near a rocky outcrop, where Jules Verne stayed for several weeks dates from the early 15th century.

The village lies along a combe formed by a bend in the White Ernz. The bell in the steeple of the parish church that calls the faithful to worship comes from the castle.

Most of the inhabitants of Larochette are of Portuguese origin. A consequence of the largest influx of immigrants in all of Europe is that more than thirty percent of the population of Luxembourg is made up of foreigners.

Aan de rand van het Müllerthal, waar een oude Karolingische wal stond, bouwde de familie von der Felz, heren van **Larochette** en als dusdanig leenroerig aan de graaf van Luxemburg, het kasteel dat zijn volle omvang kreeg in de 14de eeuw onder de Homburgs en de Crehanges. Het ging echter in de vlammen op in 1567 en werd sindsdien verwaarloosd, tot de restauratie in de jaren 1980. Het *Homburger Haus* uit het begin van de 15de eeuw ligt aan de rand van een rotsige bergtop; Jules Verne bracht er enkele weken door.

Het dorp ligt geordend in het dal dat wordt gevormd door de bocht van de witte Ernz; de klok in de klokkentoren van de parochiekerk is afkomstig van het kasteel.

De inwoners van Larochette zijn voornamelijk van Portugese afkomst; als gevolg van de grootste Europese volksverhuizing bestaat de bevolking van Luxemburg voor meer dan dertig procent uit buitenlanders.

De Larochette à Christnach, la route est bordée d'abord de rochers gris d'aspect dolomitique puis de schiste quartzeux. Le patrimoine architectural de Christnach, dont le site fut occupé dès avant notre ère, est particulièrement bien conservé. Après le village, dans la descente vers l'Ernz noire, on aperçoit le moulin à huile **'Veligsmillen'**; il est un exemple typique de l'architecture rurale du début du XIXe siècle.

Die Straße von Larochette bis Christnach ist zunächst von dolomitisch aussehenden grauen Felsen und dann von quarzhaltigem Schiefer gesäumt. Das architektonische Kunsterbe von Christnach, eines Ortes, der schon vor unserer Zeitrechnung besiedelt war, ist besonders gut erhalten. Nach dem Dorf sieht man in der Gefällstrecke zur schwarzen Ernz die Ölmühle **'Veligsmillen'**. Sie ist ein typisches Beispiel für die ländliche Architektur zu Beginn des 19. Jhs.

At first the road from Larochette to Christnach is edged with gray rocks rather like dolomite and then later with quartzose schist. The architectural heritage of Christnach, a site inhabited long before our era, is particularly well preserved. When leaving the village and descending toward the Black Ernz an oil mill called **Veligsmillen** can be seen. It is a typical example of rural architecture at the beginning of the 19th century.

De weg van Larochette naar Christnach is omzoomd met grijze rots die er eerst als dolomiet en daarna als kwartsschist uitziet. Het architecturaal erfgoed van Christnach, dat nog voor onze jaartelling bewoond was, bleef bijzonder goed bewaard. Buiten het dorp, in de afdaling naar de zwarte Ernz, duikt de oliemolen op, de felgekleurde **'Veligsmillen'**; dit is een typisch voorbeeld van de plattelandsarchitectuur van het begin van de 19de eeuw.

L'Ernz noire, avec l'Ernz blanche et la Sûre entre Reisdorf et Echternach, délimite *grosso modo* le Müllerthal. À l'origine, ce nom qui signifie 'la vallée des meuniers' désignait plus précisément celle de l'Ernz noire, ainsi nommée à cause des nombreux moulins à eau qu'elle recelait jadis. Le tourisme, qui a pris une grande extension dès le début du XXᵉ siècle, a valu à la région la dénomination de «Petite Suisse luxembourgeoise». Indûment car elle a sa propre originalité.

Dévalant en cascades écumeuses, la rivière s'encaisse au **'Schiessentümpel'**. Une passerelle en pierre s'appuie sur les rives rocheuses. De quoi enchanter les touristes anglais d'autrefois, friands de sites romantiques.

Die schwarze Ernz grenzt zusammen mit der weißen Ernz und der Sauer zwischen Reisdorf und Echternach mehr oder weniger das Müllerthal ein. Ursprünglich war das Müllerthal, das seinen Namen den zahlreichen Wassermühlen, die es dort früher gab, verdankte, das Tal der schwarzen Ernz. Der Fremdenverkehr, der Anfang des 20. Jhs. einen großen Aufschwung erlebte, trug der Region die Bezeichnung „kleine Luxemburger Schweiz" ein. Zu Unrecht, denn sie hat ihre eigenen Besonderheiten.

Der Fluss, der in schäumenden Wasserfällen hinabstürzt, verengt sich zum **'Schiessentümpel'**. Auf die felsigen Ufer stützt sich ein Steg aus Stein. Dies begeisterte früher die englischen Touristen, die romantische Orte lieben.

The Black Ernz and the White Ernz, along with the Sûre between Reisdorf and Echternach more or less delineate the Müllerthal. Originally this name, which means 'valley of the millers', meant more precisely that of the Black Ernz because of the many watermills it once had. Tourism, which increased at the beginning of the 20th century, gave the region the name of "the Luxembourg little Switzerland" which is not quite accurate as it has its own special character.

The river, hemmed in at **'Schiessentümpel'**, tumbles down in foaming waterfalls. A stone walkway clings to the riverbanks, enchanting the English tourists of bygone days, lovers of romantic sites.

De zwarte Ernz begrenst samen met de witte Ernz en de Sûre tussen Reisdorf en Echternach *grosso modo* het Müllerthal. Oorspronkelijk duidde de naam, die «Molenaarsdal» betekent, meer bepaald op de Ernz-vallei, die zo werd genoemd omwille van de vele watermolens die er eertijds stonden. Het toerisme, dat in de 20ste eeuw een hoge vlucht nam, leverde de streek de bijnaam «Luxemburgs Klein-Zwitserland» op. Helemaal terecht is dat niet, want de streek heeft een heel aparte eigenheid.

Plots stort de rivier schuimend naar beneden. We staan nu aan de **'Schiessentümpel'**, de pittoreske waterval waar een stenen bruggetje over loopt. Wat zeer in de smaak viel bij de Engelse toeristen van toen, met hun zwak voor romantische plekjes.

En territoire occupé par les Celtes avant l'invasion romaine — on y a découvert cinq espaces d'habitation et de travail —, la forteresse de **Beaufort** fut probablement édifiée au XIIᵉ siècle par Walter de Wiltz, fondateur de la seigneurie, puis renforcée au XIVᵉ siècle. Deux siècles plus tard, elle reçut sa grosse tour cylindrique et fut entourée d'une seconde enceinte. Vers la même époque, Pierre-Ernest de Mansfeld, gouverneur du duché de Luxembourg au nom du roi d'Espagne Philippe II, fit aménager deux étages résidentiels. Puis l'on construisit à partir de 1643 un confortable château Renaissance, à quelques dizaines de mètres du vieux château qui fut laissé à l'abandon.

In dem vor der römischen Invasion von den Kelten bewohnten Gebiet — es wurden dort fünf Wohn- und Arbeitsbereiche gefunden — wurde die Festung von **Beaufort** vermutlich im 12. Jh. von Walter von Wiltz, dem Gründer der Grundherrschaft, errichtet und dann im 14. Jh. erweitert. Zwei Jahrhunderte später erhielt sie ihren dicken zylindrischen Turm und wurde von einer zweiten Ringmauer umgeben. Zu derselben Zeit ließ der Gouverneur des Herzogtums Luxemburg Peter-Ernst von Mansfeld im Namen des spanischen Königs Philipp II zwei Wohnetagen einrichten. Schließlich wurde ab 1643 einige Duzend Meter vom alten Schloss, das sich selbst überlassen wurde, entfernt, ein komfortables Renaissance-Schloss gebaut.

The fortress of **Beaufort**, built around the 12th century by Walter of Wiltz, founder of the seigneury, stands in a region occupied by the Celts before the Roman invasion. Traces of five living and working emplacements have been found here. The fortress was strengthened in the 14th century. Two centuries later it acquired its massive cylindrical tower and a second set of walls. About the same time Peter Ernst von Mansfeld, Governor of the Duchy of Luxembourg for King Phillip II of Spain had two floors converted into living quarters. In 1643 construction of a comfortable Renaissance chateau began at a short distance from the old castle which was abandoned.

Op het grondgebied dat de Kelten vóór de Romeinse invasie bezetten — er werden vijf woon- en werkruimtes ontdekt — staat de vesting van **Beaufort** die wellicht in de 12de eeuw werd gebouwd door Walter van Wiltz, stichter van de heerlijkheid, en in de 14de eeuw werd versterkt. Twee eeuwen later kreeg het fort zijn cilindervormige grote toren en werd het omgeven door een tweede wal. Omstreeks die zelfde tijd liet Peter Ernest van Mansfeld, gouverneur van het hertogdom Luxemburg in naam van de Spaanse koning Filips II, er twee woonverdiepingen inrichten. Daarna werd vanaf 1643 gestart met de bouw van een comfortabel renaissance-kasteel op enkele tientallen meters van het oude kasteel dat dan links bleef liggen.

Une route sinueuse escalade le versant occidental de l'Ernz noire, en direction de Berdorf, et longe le **'Binzeltschlëff'**. Les hêtres de la forêt ajoutent à l'étrangeté du site. En certains endroits, la minceur de la couche d'humus où plongent leurs racines les oblige à se tordre parmi les rochers aux silhouettes insolites.

Double page suivante

Une conformation fissurée, crevassée, en surplomb au-dessus de la route, a suggéré aux chrétiens la comparaison avec une **chaire à prêcher**. Ils la surnommèrent le 'Predigtstuhl'.

A winding road climbs along the western slope of the Black Ernz towards Berdorf, running along the **'Binzeltschlëff'**. The beech trees of the forest add to the strange aspect of the site. In some spots the layer of humus where they are rooted is so thin that they have to twist among the unusually shaped rocks.

Next double page

A cracked and fissured formation hanging above the road led Christians to compare it with a **pulpit**, whence its name 'Prediegtstuhl'.

Eine kurvenreiche Straße führt den westlichen Hang der schwarzen Ernz am **'Binzeltschlëff'** entlang in Richtung Berdorf hinauf. Die Buchen des Waldes tragen zum eigentümlichen Charakter des Ortes bei. An einigen Stellen werden sie durch die dünne Humusschicht, in die sie ihre Wurzeln strecken, dazu gezwungen, sich zwischen den Felsen mit den ungewöhnlichen Silhouetten hindurchzuwinden.

Folgende Doppelseite

Eine die Straße überragende zerklüftete Formation erhielt von den Christen den Beinamen ,**Predigtstuhl**'.

Een kronkelende weg beklimt de westelijke helling van de zwarte Ernz in de richting van Berdorf, en loopt langs de **'Binzeltschlëff'**. De beuken van het woud dompelen de plek in een vreemde sfeer. Her en der is de humuslaag waar hun wortels in zitten zo dun dat ze zich een weg moeten banen tussen de grillige rotsen.

Volgende dubbele pagina

Een gespleten, gekloofde rotsformatie die over de weg hangt, roept bij christenen het beeld op van een preekstoel. De rotspartij kreeg dan ook de bijnaam **'Predigtstuhl'**.

155

Ci-dessus et page 160

Le climat aidant, l'érosion a fait œuvre de sculpteur dans le Müllerthal. L'eau de la pluie, des sources et des ruisseaux a pénétré dans les anfractuosités de la pierre. Le gel a fait éclater le grès poreux et des pans de roche se sont écartés des collines, glissant progressivement dans les ravins.

Véritable labyrinthe, le massif gréseux du **'Weerschrumschlëff'** est creusé d'étroites failles aux falaises parallèles. Le promeneur qui s'y engage, s'y faufile, ne manque pas d'être fortement impressionné.

Oben und Seite 160

Unter Einwirkung des Klimas hat sich die Erosion im Müllerthal als Bildhauer betätigt. Das Wasser des Regens, der Quellen und der Bäche ist in die Struktur des Steins eingedrungen. Der Frost hat den porösen Sandstein dann zum Bersten gebracht, so dass Felsteile sich von den Hügeln abgelöst haben und allmählich in die Schluchten abgeglitten sind.

Das Sandsteinmassiv der **'Weerschrumschlëff'**, ein regelrechtes Labyrinth, ist in Verwerfungen an den parallelen Felswänden gegraben. Der Spaziergänger, der dort hineingeht und sich dort hindurchschlängelt, wird in jedem Falle tief beeindruckt sein.

Above and following page

Because of climatic conditions, erosion has played a role in sculpting the Müllerthal. Springs, streams and rain have penetrated into crevices in the stone. Frost has split the porous sandstone and sheets of rock have broken from the hills, sliding slowly down into the ravines.

The sandstone massif of the **'Weerschrumschlëff'** is a veritable labyrinth, tunneled by narrow faults with parallel cliffs. The hiker who ventures into it cannot help but be overawed.

Hierboven en volgende pagina

Met de hulp van het klimaat ging de erosie aan het beeldhouwen in het Müllerthal. Het water van de regen, van de bronnen en van de beekjes drong in de rotsspleten. Vorst deed het poreuze gres barsten en stukken rots kwamen los van de heuvels en gleden geleidelijk in de ravijnen.

Het zandsteenachtig massief van de **'Weerschrumschlëff'** is een heuse doolhof met nauwe kloven en evenwijdige kliffen. De wandelaar die er zich waagt, er zich een weg zoekt, zal beslist zeer onder de indruk komen.

Ci-dessus

Á Berdorf, du haut du **belvédère de Roitzbach** et du '**Nid d'aigle**', on a vue sur l'apaisante partie des vallées de l'Ernz noire et du Halerbaach qui se rencontrent plus de cent-cinquante mètres en contrebas.

Ci-dessous et double page suivante

Parcouru de ruisselets et de petits torrents, jalonné de ravins abrupts entre des pans de rochers en grès, le Müllerthal joint à la sauvagerie romantique un mystère à nul autre pareil, vecteur de légendes et de récits fantastiques. Depuis Berdorf, **l'Aesbaach** dévale une gorge creusée de cavernes spacieuses, semée de blocs auxquels l'érosion a donné des formes bizarres, avant de se jeter dans la Sûre en amont d'Echternach.

Oben

In Berdorf hat man oben vom **Aussichtspunkt von Roitzbach** und vom „**Adlerhorst**' aus eine Aussicht über den ruhigen Teil der Täler der schwarzen Ernz und des Halerbaach, die mehr als 150 Meter weiter unten aufeinander treffen.

Unten und folgende Doppelseite

Bei dem von Bächen und kleinen Wildwassern durchzogenen und von steilen Schluchten zwischen Sandstein-Felsbrocken gesäumten Müllerthal kommt zu der romantischen Unberührtheit ein unvergleichlicher geheimnisvoller Charakter hinzu, aus dem Legenden und fantastische Geschichten entstanden sind. Von Berdorf aus stürzt **der Aesbaach** eine von großen Höhlen durchzogene Schlucht hinunter, welche von Blöcken gesäumt ist, denen die Erosion seltsame Formen gegeben hat, um dann oberhalb von Echternach in die Sauer zu fließen.

Above

From the heights of the **Eagle's Nest** at Berdorf one has a prospect of the more serene part of the valleys of the Black Ernz and of the Halerbaach that join together more than one hundred and fifty meters below.

Right and next double page

The Müllerthal, traversed by brooks and small torrents, studded with steep ravines between sections of sandstone, conjoins a romantic wildness with a unique mysteriousness, which has given rise to many legends and fantastic tales. After Berdorf, **the Aesbaach** tumbles through a gorge hollowed out with large caves and sprinkled with rocks eroded into bizarre shapes before joining the Sûre upstream from Echternach.

Hierboven

In Berdorf biedt de **belvédère van Roitsbach** en het hoger gelegen '**Arendsnest**', een mooi uitzicht op het vredige deel van de valleien van de zwarte Ernz en van de Halerbaach die elkaar meer dan honderd vijftig meter lager treffen.

Links en volgende dubbele pagina

Het Müllerthal wordt doorkruist door vlietende beekjes en stroompjes en is bestrooid met steile ravijnen tussen stukken rots van zandsteen. Zijn wilde en tegelijk romantische aanblik ademt een geheimzinnige sfeer als nergens anders, een vruchtbare voedingsbodem voor legendes en fantastische verhalen. Van Berdorf stort **de Aesbaach** zich in een gleuf met weidse grotten — die bezaaid zijn met blokken waar de erosie bizarre vormen in houwde — alvorens zich in de Süre te storten, stroomopwaarts van Echternach.

À l'entrée de la partie la plus étroite de la gorge de l'Aesbaach, non loin de la route de Berdorf à Echternach, se trouve un rocher turriculé. Il a été surnommé la '**tour Malakoff**' par allusion à l'ouvrage défensif qui protégeait Sébastopol pendant la guerre de Crimée et fut pris par le maréchal Mac-Mahon le 8 septembre 1855. Celui-ci y déclara «J'y suis, j'y reste».

Am Eingang des schmalsten Teils der Aesbaach-Schlucht, nicht weit von der Straße von Berdorf nach Echternach entfernt, befindet sich der '**Malakoff-Turm**'. Seinen Namen verdankt er dem Verteidigungswerk, das Sewastopol während des Krim-Kriegs schützte und am 8. September 1855 von Marschall Mac-Mahon eingenommen wurde, der dort erklärte: „Hier bin ich, hier bleibe ich."

At the entrance to the narrowest part of the Aesbaach gorge, not far from the Berdorf to Echternach road, there is turreted rock with whorls forming a high, conical spiral. It has been nicknamed the **Malakoff Tower**, a reference to the fortifications protecting Sevastopol during the Crimean war, captured by Marshal Mac-Mahon on September 8, 1855. The Marshal declared "Here I am and here I stay".

Aan de ingang van het smalste deel van de engte van de Aesbaach, niet ver van de weg van Berdorf naar Echternach, is een torenvormige rots te vinden. Deze kreeg de naam '**Malakoff-toren**' als verwijzing naar het defensiewerk dat Sebastopol beschermde tijdens de Krimoorlog en dat werd ingenomen door maarschalk Mac-Mahon op 8 september 1855. Hij verklaarde er «Ik ben er, ik blijf er».

Les parois de la 'gorge du Loup'
longue de 150 mètres et haute de
50 sont d'une verticalité impres-
sionnante. Il n'est pas surprenant
que les légendes abondent dans la
région, notamment celle de la
«chanteuse du Müllerthal», jeune
princesse favorite de la fée de la
musique. Elle attirait les chevaliers
par son chant. L'un d'entre eux,
dans sa hâte de la rejoindre, disparut dans un gouffre ; elle en mourut de chagrin mais, une fois l'an,
sortait de sa tombe et chantait
pour son amoureux. Ceux qui
n'étaient pas ravis par sa voix se
transformaient en pierres déchi-
quetées...

Die Wände der 150 Meter langen
und 50 Meter hohen 'Wolfsschlucht' sind von eindrucksvoller
Vertikalität. Da überrascht es
nicht, dass es in der Region zahlreiche Legenden gibt, insbesondere die
der „Sängerin des Müllerthals", der
jungen Lieblingsprinzessin der
Musikfee, die die Ritter mit ihrem
Gesang lockte. Einer der Ritter verschwand in seiner Eile, zu ihr zu
gelangen, in einer Schlucht. Sie
starb vor Kummer dran, stieg aber
einmal im Jahr aus ihrem Grab
und sang für ihren Geliebten. Wer
von ihrer Stimme nicht entzückt
war, verwandelte sich in einen zer-
klüfteten Stein...

The walls of the **Wolf's gorge**,
150 meters long and 50 meters
high are remarkably steep. It is not
surprising that legends abound in
the region, notably that of the
"songstress of Müllerthal", a
young princess favoured by the
music fairy. She attracted knights
with her singing. One of them, in
his haste to join her, disappeared
into an abyss. She died of sorrow
but once a year, rises from her
grave and sings for her suitors.
Those who are not enchanted by
her voice are changed into jagged
stones...

De wanden van de 'Wolfs-
schlucht', de «Wolfskloof», die 150
meter lang en 50 meter hoog is,
zijn opmerkelijk verticaal. Het zal
niemand verbazen dat de legendes
in deze streek welig tieren, zoals
het verhaal van de 'zangeres van het
Müllerthal', de favoriete jonge prinses van de fee van de muziek. Zij
lokte de ridders met haar gezang.
Één van hen verdween, in zijn haast
om haar te vervoegen, in een kloof;
zij stierf van verdriet, maar één keer
per jaar staat ze op uit haar graf om
voor haar geliefde te zingen. Wie
niet ingenomen is met haar stem,
verandert in verkruimelde steen...

▲▶▶

La comtesse Ermesinde donna le droit de cité à **Echternach** dès 1236. Sur la **place du Marché** où une croix de Justice rappelle ce privilège, le Dënzelt (1520-1530), ancien siège du tribunal médiéval, s'avance au-dessus d'une galerie à solides arcades gothiques. Deux échauguettes flanquent le sommet de la façade qui est ornée de six statues. Elles représentent la Vierge et Salomon au centre, la Tempérance, la Justice, la Prudence et le Courage sur les côtés. La place est entièrement fermée par des maisons patriciennes et nobles. Celle dénommée 'Sous les portiques' fait face au Dënzelt ; elle faisait jadis office d'hôtel de ville.

Countess Ermesinde granted civil rights to **Echternach** in 1236. On the **Market Square** where a Justice Cross recalls this privilege is the Dënzelt (1520-1530), formerly the seat of the mediaeval court, projecting above a gallery of sturdy Gothic arches. Two watchtowers flank the top of the façade decorated with six statues, representing the Virgin and Solomon in the centre surrounded by Temperance, Justice, Prudence and Courage. The square is completely closed in by the houses of nobles and patricians. One called "Under the Porticos", facing the Dënzelt, was once the Town Hall.

Gräfin Ermesinde gab **Echternach** im Jahre 1236 die Stadtrechte. Auf dem **Marktplatz**, auf dem ein Justizkreuz an dieses Privileg erinnert, springt der Dënzelt (1520-1530), der ehemalige Sitz des mittelalterlichen Gerichts, über einer Galerie mit soliden gotischen Arkaden hervor. Zwei Warten umgeben die Spitze der mit sechs Statuen geschmückten Fassade. In der Mitte sind die Heilige Jungfrau und Salomon und an den Seiten die Mäßigkeit, die Gerechtigkeit, die Umsicht und die Kraft zu sehen. Der Platz wird vollständig von den Häusern von Patriziern und Adeligen geschlossen. Gegenüber vom Dënzelt befindet sich ein ‚Unter den Steilen' genanntes Haus, das einst als Rathaus diente.

Gravin Ermesinde verleende **Echternach** burgerrechten in 1236. Op het marktplein, de **place du Marché**, waar een gerechtskruis aan dit privilege herinnert, steekt de Dënzelt (1520-1530), het voormalige middeleeuwse gerechtsgebouw, uit boven een galerij met stevige gotische bogen. Twee wachttorentjes flankeren de top van de gevel die met zes beelden getooid is. Ze stellen in het midden de Maagd Maria en Salomon voor, de Soberheid, de Gerechtigheid, de Voorzichtigheid en de Dapperheid aan de zijkanten. Het plein is helemaal omsloten door woningen van patriciërs en edelen. Het zogenoemde huis 'Sous les portiques' staat tegenover de Dënzelt; het diende vroeger als stadhuis.

▲▶
Du haut du Trooskneppchen, à l'issue de la promenade de la gorge du Loup, **Echternach** laisse d'emblée deviner la richesse de ses monuments. Le nom de *villa Epternacum* apparaît pour la première fois à la fin du VIIe siècle, c'est-à-dire à l'époque de la fondation d'une abbaye bénédictine confiée à saint Willibrord.

Les premiers éléments de l'enceinte furent érigés au temps des invasions normandes ; ils furent ensuite renforcés aux XIe et XIIe siècles. L'enceinte avait alors un développement d'environ deux kilomètres et comportait une vingtaine de tours du type «la gorge ouverte», non-fermées du côté de la ville. Huit d'entre elles sont conservées.

Nach dem Spaziergang in der Wolfsschlucht lässt sich oben vom Trooskneppchen aus bereits die Vielfalt der Monumente von **Echternach** ahnen. Der Name *Villa Epternacum* wird erstmals Ende des 7. Jhs. erwähnt, das heißt zur Zeit der Gründung einer Benediktinerabtei, die dem Heiligen Willibrord anvertraut wurde.

Die ersten Elemente der Schutzmauer wurden zur Zeit der normannischen Invasionen errichtet. Anschließend wurde sie im 11. und 12. Jh. verstärkt. Die Schutzmauer war damals ungefähr zwei Kilometer lang und umfasste rund 20 zur Stadt hin offene Türme. Acht von ihnen sind erhalten geblieben.

After walking through the Wolf's gorge to the heights of Trooskneppchen, one sees the rich heritage of monuments in **Echternach** lying below. The name of *villa Epternacum* appears for the first time at the end of the 7th century, that is at the period when the Benedictine abbey entrusted to Saint Willibrord was founded.

The first set of walls was built at the time of the Viking invasions and strengthened during the 11th and 12th centuries. The walls then were about two kilometres around and had some twenty "open throat" towers that are open on the city side. Eight are still standing.

Op de top van de Trooskneppchen, na de wandeling door de 'Wolfsschlucht', spreidt **Echternach** meteen de rijkdom van zijn monumenten ten toon. De naam *villa Epternacum* is voor het eerst te vinden op het eind van de zevende eeuw, dit wil zeggen in de tijd van de stichting van een benedictijnerabdij die aan Sint Willibrord werd toevertrouwd.

De eerste elementen van de omwalling werden gebouwd tijdens de invasies van de Noormannen; ze werden nadien versterkt in de elfde en in de twaalfde eeuw. De walmuur was toen ongeveer twee kilometer lang en omvatte een twintigtal torens met een 'open keel' naar de stad toe. Acht daarvan zijn nog bewaard.

L'**abbaye d'Echternach** constituait une ville dans la ville. Il ne subsiste aucune trace des premiers bâtiments. Construite en 1727, l'abbaye se compose de quatre ailes de bâtiments fort sobres, de style dit Marie-Thérèse, enfermant une cour carrée. Ils sont aujourd'hui occupés par le lycée. Plus austères que l'abbaye, les dépendances (*ci-dessus*) sont empreintes d'une exceptionnelle harmonie architecturale.

Devenue l'une des plus rayonnantes institutions monastiques d'Europe occidentale, l'abbaye d'Echternach abrita, durant tout le moyen âge, un *scriptorium* d'où sortirent des chefs-d'œuvre de l'art du manuscrit et de l'enluminure.

Die **Abtei von Echternach** bildete eine Stadt in der Stadt. Von den ersten Gebäuden sind keine Spuren erhalten. Die 1727 erbaute Abtei besteht aus vier sehr nüchternen Gebäudeflügeln im Stil von Maria Theresia, die einen eckigen Hof umgeben. Heute ist das Gymnasium darin untergebracht. Die Nebengebäude (*oben*), die schlichter sind als die Abtei, sind von einer außergewöhnlichen architektonischen Harmonie geprägt.

Die zu einer der strahlendsten Klostereinrichtungen Westeuropas gewordene Abtei von Echternach beherbergte im gesamten Mittelalter ein *Scriptorium*, aus dem Meisterwerke der Kunst der Handschrift und der Buchmalerei hervorgingen.

The **Abbey of Echternach** was a city within a city. Nothing remains of the first buildings. The present Abbey, built in 1727, is made up of four wings surrounding a square courtyard in the restrained Maria Theresa style is now a secondary school. The outbuildings (*above*) are more austere than the Abbey and present an exceptional architectural harmony.

The Abbey of Echternach became one of the most influential monastic establishments of Western Europe, sheltering during the length of the Middle Ages a *scriptorium* producing masterpieces in the art of manuscripts and illuminations.

De **abdij van Echternach** was een stad in de stad. Er rest geen enkel spoor meer van de eerste gebouwen. De abdij werd gebouwd in 1727 en bestaat uit vier vleugels met zeer eenvoudige gebouwen, in de zogenaamde Maria-Theresiastijl en rond een vierkante binnenplaats. Er huist momenteel een lyceum. De bijgebouwen (*hierboven*) ogen strenger dan de abdij en dragen de stempel van een uitzonderlijke architecturale harmonie.

De abdij van Echternach groeide uit tot een kloosterinstelling met bijzonder veel weerklank in West-Europa en huisvestte de hele Middeleeuwen door een *scriptorium* dat ware meesterwerken van de handschrift- en de verluchtingskunst afleverde.

Ci-dessus et ci-dessous

La vie monastique au XVIIIᵉ siècle avait perdu sa rigueur d'antan. À **Echternach**, les moines accueillaient de plus en plus d'hôtes de marque. À leur intention, l'abbé Grégoire aménagea un jardin de plaisance à la française. L'**orangerie** (1735-1736), à laquelle on accède en franchissant une grille en fer forgé, hébergeait ces hôtes de l'abbaye. Les statues qui animent la façade représentent allégoriquement les quatre saisons.

Double page suivante

Dans le parc de l'abbaye, non loin de la berge de la Sûre, le **'pavillon des évêques'** (1761-1765) de style Louis XV s'élève en gracieuse rotonde, précédé d'un parterre dessiné à la française avec raffinement. On y déjeunait et conversait.

Oben und unten

Das Klosterleben im 18. Jh. hatte seine einstige Strenge verloren. In **Echternach** beherbergten die Mönche immer mehr vornehme Gäste. Für sie legte Abt Gregor einen Lustgarten nach französischem Vorbild an. Diese Gäste der Abtei wurden in der **Orangerie** (1735-1736), zu der man durch ein schmiedeeisernes Gitter gelangt, beherbergt. Die Statuen, die die Fassade beleben, stellen in allegorischer Weise die vier Jahreszeiten dar.

Folgende Doppelseite

Im Park der Abtei, nicht weit vom Ufer der Sauer entfernt, erhebt sich in eleganter Rotunde der **,Pavillon der Bischöfe'** (1761-1765) im Stil Ludwig XV, vor dem sich ein raffiniert französisch gestaltetes Blumenbeet befindet. Im Pavillon wurde zu Mittag gegessen und Konversation gemacht.

Above and below

Monastic life in the 18th century was less strict than in bygone days. The monks of **Echternach** received more and more prominent guests. To this purpose, Abbot Gregory installed a formal garden in the French style with an orangery and a pavilion. The abbey guests lodged in the **orangery**, entered by a gate in wrought iron. The statues decorating the façade are allegories of the four seasons.

Following double page

The **Bishops' Pavilion** (1761-1765), a graceful rotunda in the Louis XV style, stands in the abbey park, not far from the banks of the Sûre. Elegant flowerbeds in the French style lie before it. Here one dined and conversed.

Hierboven en -onder

Het kloosterleven was in de 18de eeuw lang niet meer zo strikt. In **Echternach** onthaalden de monniken meer en meer gasten met naam. Voor hen richtte abt Grégoire een lusttuin in Franse stijl in, met een orangerie en een paviljoen. De **orangerie** (1735-1736), die toegankelijk is langs een hek van ijzersmeedwerk, herbergde deze gasten van de abdij. De beelden die de gevel sieren, verzinnebeelden de vier seizoenen.

Dubbele volgende pagina

In het park van de abdij, niet ver van de oever van de Sûre, prijkt het **'paviljoen van de bisschoppen'** (1761-1765), een sierlijke rotonde in Lodewijk XV-stijl, voorafgegaan door een bloemperk naar een verfijnd Frans ontwerp. Er werd gegeten en gepraat.

La route du vin
Die Weinstraße

De Schengen à Wasserbillig, la Moselle traverse un plateau peu élevé. L'excellente orientation des versants de la vallée et des coteaux alentours jointe à la relative douceur du climat incita les Romains à y aménager des vignobles. Avec un succès que le poète Anconius célébra sous le titre *Mosella*. Au moyen âge, les moines prirent le relais et, avec des hauts et des bas, la viticulture s'est poursuivie jusqu'à aujourd'hui.

Von Schengen bis Wasserbillig durchfließt die Mosel ein niedrig gelegenes Plateau. Die ausgezeichnete Lage der Hänge des Tals und der umliegenden Anhöhen sowie der vergleichsweise gemäßigte Charakter des Klimas veranlassten die Römer dazu, dort ihre Weinberge anzulegen. Den Erfolg pries der Dichter Anconius in seinem Werk *Mosella*. Im Mittelalter traten die Mönche die Nachfolge an. Bis heute wurde der Weinbau — mit Höhen und Tiefen — fortgeführt.

The Wine Road
De wijnroute

The Moselle crosses a low plateau from Schengen to Wasserbillig. The excellent orientation of the valley slopes and the surrounding hillsides, along with the relatively mild climate persuaded the Romans to plant vineyards. These proved so successful that the poet Anconius praised them in his work entitled Mosella. The monks took over during the Middle Ages and cultivation, with ups and downs, has continued until.

Van Schengen naar Wasserbillig doorkruist de Moezel een vrij laag plateau. De uitstekende ligging van de heuvelflanken en van de heuvels in de omgeving, gekoppeld aan de betrekkelijke zachtheid van het klimaat brachten de Romeinen op het idee om er wijngaarden aan te leggen. Met een succes dat de dichter Anconius bezong onder de titel Mosella. In de middeleeuwen namen de monniken de fakkel over van een wijnbouw die, met hoogtes en laagtes, tot op vandaag wordt voortgezet.

Le paysage depuis les hauteurs de **Wellen** en Allemagne, rappelle que la Moselle, tout comme l'Our, constitue une frontière naturelle entre les deux pays. Au temps de l'Union douanière avec la Prusse, 80 pour cent du vin luxembourgeois était exporté en Allemagne, non pas pour être dégusté mais pour servir de vin de coupage. L'Union économique belgo-luxembourgeoise de 1921 modifia les perspectives et la plupart des vignerons se regroupèrent en coopératives. Elles améliorent les techniques de production et de commercialisation de vins capables désormais de rivaliser avec ceux de l'étranger bénéficiant d'une grande renommée.

Triple page suivante

Les vignobles mosellans — tels ceux de **Wintrange** —recouvrent 1 300 hectares cultivés par quelque 900 vignerons.

Above

The countryside as seen from the heights of **Wellen** in Germany shows that the Moselle, like the Our, forms a natural frontier between the two countries. During the period of the Customs Union with Prussia, 80% of the wine of Luxembourg was exported to Germany, not for drinking but for blending. The Belgian-Luxembourg Economic Union Of 1921 changed this practice. Most of the winegrowers formed cooperatives, improving production techniques and commercialization. The result is a product now capable of competing with the most illustrious wines produced in other countries.

Next triple page

The Moselle vineyards, such as those of **Wintrange** cover 1,300 hectares and are cultivated by around 900 winegrowers.

Oben

Von den Höhen von **Wellen** in Deutschland aus erinnert die Landschaft daran, dass die Mosel ebenso wie die Our eine natürliche Grenze zwischen den beiden Ländern darstellt. Zu Zeiten der Zollunion mit Preußen wurden 80 Prozent des luxemburgischen Weins nach Deutschland exportiert, nicht um dort verkostet zu werden, sondern um als Verschnittwein zu dienen. Die belgisch-luxemburgische Wirtschaftsunion von 1921 änderte die Perspektiven, und die meisten Winzer schlossen sich zu Genossenschaften zusammen. Sie verbesserten die Produktions- und Vertriebstechniken der Weine, die seither mit renommierten ausländischen Weinen konkurrieren können.

Folgende Dreifachseite

Die Moselweinberge — wie die von **Wintrange** — bedecken 1.300 Hektar, die von rund 900 Winzern bestellt werden.

Hierboven

Het landschap dat van op de hoogtes van **Wellen** in Duitsland te zien is, herinnert eraan dat de Moezel, net als de Our, een natuurlijke grens is tussen beide landen. In de tijd van de Douane-unie met Pruisen, werd 80 % van de Luxemburgse wijn uitgevoerd naar Duitsland, niet om rechtstreeks in het glas te komen, maar om te versnijden. De Belgisch-Luxemburgse Economische Unie uit 1921 wijzigde de perspectieven en de meeste wijnbouwers verenigden zich in coöperatieven. Ze verbeteren de productie- en commercialiseringstechnieken van wijnen die nu best kunnen wedijveren met vermaarde buitenlandse wijnen uit het buitenland.

Volgende driedubbele pagina

De wijngaarden van de Moezel — zoals van **Wintrange** — beslaan 1 300 hectare die door ongeveer 900 wijnbouwers worden verbouwd.

Pages 183 à 187

Construit principalement aux XVIe et XVIIe siècles, **Wellenstein** est situé au milieu des vignobles du Rülander et du Traminer, à un kilomètre à l'ouest de la Moselle, «à l'intérieur du pays» serait-on tenté d'écrire, tant cet affluent du Rhin semble une frontière naturelle quasi infranchissable en comparaison avec les autres cours d'eau du pays.

La restauration du village est exemplaire. Dans l'étroite impasse conduisant à l'auberge de jeunesse, les arcades soutenant les façades opposées ont été maintenues. Près de l'église, les anciennes maisons de viticulteurs ont conservé leur bâti traditionnel assez trapu, coiffé d'une toiture à pente douce faite de tuiles canal qui leur confère un charme méridional.

Seite 183 bis 187

Das insbesondere im 16. und 17. Jh. erbaute **Wellenstein** liegt inmitten der Rülander- und Traminer-Weinberge, einen Kilometer westlich von der Mosel, „im Landesinnern", ist man versucht zu schreiben, so sehr scheint dieser Zufluss des Rheins im Vergleich zu den übrigen Wasserläufen des Landes eine natürliche, nahezu nicht zu überschreitende Grenze zu bilden.

Die Restaurierung des Dorfes ist beispielhaft. In der engen Sackgasse, die zur Jugendherberge führt, sind die Arkaden, die die gegenüber liegenden Fassaden stützen, noch vorhanden. In der Nähe der Kirche ist die recht wuchtige traditionelle Bauform der ehemaligen Winzerhäuser erhalten. Sie sind mit einem sanft geneigten Dach aus Kanalziegeln gedeckt, das ihnen einen südländischen Charme verleiht.

Pages 183 to 187

Wellenstein, built mainly in the 16th and 17th centuries, is situated in the middle of the Rülander and Traminer vineyards, about a kilometre west of the Moselle. One is tempted to say it is in the interior of the country, as the tributary of the Rhine seems like a nearly impassable natural frontier when compared to the other rivers of the country.

The village has been impeccably restored. In the narrow dead-end street leading to the youth hostel the arches supporting the opposing façades of the houses have been maintained. Near the church the squat old houses of the winegrowers with their gently sloping roofs in curved tiles such as those of the Midi, retain their original character.

Pagina 183 tot 187

Wellenstein werd grotendeels gebouwd in de 16de en in de 17de eeuw en ligt midden in de wijngaarden van de Rülander en de Traminer, op een kilometer ten westen van de Moezel, "in het binnenland" zou men bijna schrijven, zodanig lijkt deze bijrivier van de Rijn een natuurlijke grens te vormen waar bijna niet over te komen is, vergeleken met de andere waterlopen van het land.

De restauratie van het dorp is werkelijk voorbeeldig. In het doodlopend steegje dat naar de jeugdherberg leidt, werden de bogen die de gevels tegenover elkaar steunen bewaard. Bij de kerk zien de oude woningen van de wijnbouwers er nog steeds traditioneel uit, vrij gedrongen, met een zachthellend dak van Romeinse dakpannen die ze een zuiderse charme verlenen.

▲▼▶ **Ehnen** et les villages voisins formaient la Cour de Lenningen qui appartenait au Grand Chapitre de l'archevêché de Trèves. Le bourg était le centre administratif de la Cour, s'y trouvaient la grange au dîmes et la résidence de l'écoutète — le procureur, en termes d'aujourd'hui. Ses maisons ont gardé leur caractère ancien. En témoignent, parmi d'autres, l'«Al Schoumesch», maison mosellane de type roman avec portail d'entrée, la petite maison des sœurs grises de Trèves aménagée en grange, l'«Hietebau» avec passage couvert, le «Dommherrenbau», ancien moulin loué à bail par le Grand Chapitre de Trèves transformé en élégante demeure patricienne.

Ehnen und die umliegenden Dörfer bildeten den Hof von Lenningen, der zum Großen Kapitel des Erzbistums Trier gehörte. Der Marktflecken war das Verwaltungszentrum des Hofes. Dort befanden sich die Zehntscheune und die Residenz des Schultheißes — des heutigen Staatsanwalts. Die Häuser haben ihren früheren Charakter bewahrt. Davon zeugen unter anderem das moselaner Haus romanischen Stils mit Eingangstor 'Al Schoumesch', das zu einer Scheune umgebaute kleine Haus der Grauen Schwestern von Trier 'Hietebau' mit bedecktem Übergang und der ,Dommherrenbau', eine alte vom Großen Kapitel von Trier gemietete ehemalige Mühle, die zu einem eleganten Patrizierhaus umgebaut wurde.

Ehnen and the surrounding villages formed the Court of Lenningen that belonged to the Grand Chapter of the Archbishopric of Trier. The town was the Court administrative centre with a tithe barn and the residence of the prosecutor. The houses have retained their old aspect, for example, the 'Al Sschoumesch', a typical mosellan Romanesque house with a portal. Others are the little house of the Grey Nuns of Trier, now a barn, the 'Hietebau' with its covered passage and the 'Dommherrenbau', formerly a mill rented out by the Grand Chapter of Trier and now converted into an elegant patrician residence.

Ehnen en zijn buurdorpen vormden het Hof van Lenningen dat deel uitmaakte van het Groot-Kapittel van de aartsbisschop van Trier. Het stadje was het administratief centrum van het Hof, met de tiendenschuur en de residentie van de schout — de procureur, zoals hij nu heet. De huizen bewaarden hun vroegere karakter. Daarvan getuigen onder meer 'Al Schoumesch', een Moezel-huis in romaanse stijl met ingangsportaal, het kleine huis van de grijze zusters van Trier dat als schuur werd ingericht, de 'Hietebau' met een overdekte doorgang, de 'Dommherrenbau', de oude molen die verhuurd wordt door het Groot-Kapittel van Trier en werd omgebouwd tot elegante patriciërswoning.

▲▶

Séduisante dans sa simplicité, l'«A Champans», maison construite à **Ehnen** en 1592, présente de beaux arcs en pierre au-dessus des portes et fenêtres.

Das in seiner Einfachheit bezaubernde 'A Champans', ein 1592 in **Ehnen** errichtetes Haus, weist über den Türen und Fenstern schöne Steinbögen auf.

'A Champans', a charmingly simple house built in **Ehnen** in 1592, has handsome stone arches above the doors and windows.

Bekoorlijk door zijn eenvoud is het 'A Champans', een huis dat in 1592 werd gebouwd in **Ehnen**, met mooie stenen bogen boven de ramen en deuren.

190

Les trois chérubins de la «**fontaine aux raisins**» **à Schwebsange** se prélassent parmi les grappes de raisin, qui les couvrent à foison et débordent du petit monument. Deux d'entre eux tiennent le flacon de vin qui leur procure joie et euphorie. Sculpturale invitation adressée aux Mosellans qui les imitent une fois l'an, lorsqu'ils fêtent la fin des vendanges et que, de la fontaine, le vin coule à flot...

Die drei Cherubinen des ‚**Weinbrunnens' in Schwebsange** machen es sich in den Weintrauben bequem, die sie überwuchern und über das kleine Denkmal hinausreichen. Zwei von ihnen halten die Weinflasche, die ihnen Freude und Euphorie beschert. Eine bildhauerische Einladung an die Moselaner, die sie einmal im Jahr imitieren, wenn sie das Ende der Ernte feiern und der Wein in Strömen aus dem Brunnen fließt...

The three cherubs of the '**grape fountain' in Schwebsange** frolic amid abundant bunches of grapes that spill out of the little monument. Two of them hold the wine flasks that contribute to their joy and euphoria. This is a sculptural invitation to the Mosellans who imitate them once a year during the grape harvest festival when wine flows from the fountain.

De drie engelen van de '**druivenfontein' in Schwebsange** laten zich helemaal gaan tussen de weelderige druiventrossen die hen bijna volledig bedekken en tot over de rand van het kleine monument gaan. Twee ervan houden een wijnflacon in de hand die ze blijkbaar levenslustig en euforisch maakt. Het is een heuse uitnodiging in steen aan de Moezelbewoners die ze één keer per jaar nadoen, als ze het oogstfeest vieren en de fontein gul wijn spuit...

ℋ VINCENT MERCKX

E D I T I O N S

2004 © s.p.r.l. Editions Merckx Uitgeverij b.v.b.a.
Avenue des Statuaires 145A, B-1180 Bruxelles
Beeldhouwerslaan 145A, B-1180 Brussel

☎ +32/2/374.41.56 • Fax +32/2/375.80.37
info@merckxeditions.com
www.merckxeditions.com

Nederlandse bewerking & Deutsche Übersetzung	DSDB
English translation	Sheila Tessier-Lavigne
Typesetting	Deloge
Photoengraving	Steurs
Printing	Daneels

D-2003-0398-33
ISBN 90-74847-33-1